Hearts
on Fire

Hearts
on Fire

Praying with Jesuits

Edited by
Michael Harter, SJ

LOYOLA PRESS.
A JESUIT MINISTRY

Chicago

For the name of someone in your area from whom you could obtain further information about the Jesuits or with whom you could discuss the possibility of becoming a Jesuit, please write or call:

Vocation Director
Jesuit Conference
1616 P Street NW, Suite 300
Washington, DC 20036-1420
(202) 462-0400

LOYOLA PRESS.
A JESUIT MINISTRY

3441 N. Ashland Avenue
Chicago, Illinois 60657
(800) 621-1008
www.loyolapress.com

Originally published by the Institute of Jesuit Sources, St. Louis, MO, in 1993 under ISBN 1-880810-04-2. Reprinted by permission of the Institute of Jesuit Sources.

Cover design by Kathryn Seckman Kirsch
Interior design by Arc Group Ltd

Library of Congress Cataloging-in-Publication Data
Hearts on fire : praying with Jesuits / edited by Michael Harter.

      p. cm.
    Originally published: St. Louis, Mo. : Institute of Jesuit Sources, 1993.
    Includes index.
    ISBN-13: 978-0-8294-2120-0; ISBN-10: 0-8294-2120-3
  1. Jesuits—Prayer-books and devotions—English. 2. Catholic Church—Prayer-books and devotions—English. I. Harter, Michael.
BX2050.J47H43 2004
242'.802—dc22

                                     2004019769

Printed in the United States of America
15 16 17 18 Bang 14 13 12 11 10

Contents

Prayers for the Start of the Day

Devotional Materials

Introduction

Were not our hearts on fire?" the two disciples of Jesus are reported by Luke (24:32) to have said to each other as they hurried back to Jerusalem to relate to their friends what had happened to them in the village of Emmaus. What the disciples told their companions about their experience and what they in turn heard from their friends about their own encounters with the resurrected Jesus deepened their faith and enabled them to carry on with renewed energy and hope. (See Luke 24:13–35 for the whole story.)

Those who ponder Scripture know that what those disciples experienced can happen to any Christian who searches for a closer relationship with the Lord. When a person explores his or her deepest desires or questions—and talks about them with someone else who is on a similar journey—each person in the conversation receives new understanding, new insight.

From the time of Ignatius to the present day, Jesuits have prayed the Scriptures. Their hearts, too, have been set on fire, and they have shared their insights and questions with their companions and friends. They have taught classes, preached sermons, directed retreats. They have distilled their struggles, questions, and wisdom into journals and books. From such sources the prayers in this book have been gleaned.

St. Ignatius of Loyola (1491–1556), the founder of the Society of Jesus, kept a little notebook in which he recorded some of his favorite prayers. In that same book he also jotted down some exercises that he found helpful and outlined some reflections that were important for him during the time of his conversion. These notes make up the heart of what we now call the Spiritual Exercises. The prayers in this book are arranged so that they can be a companion to those exercises or simply used to focus the events of daily life.

The exercises are divided into four parts, which are commonly referred to as "weeks" even though there are no fixed number of days in each section. The full experience of the exercises usually takes about thirty days to complete— and a lifetime to assimilate.

All the prayers in this book are by Jesuits. Some are direct paraphrases of material in the exercises; others are practical applications of the exercises. Other than a general grouping of prayers according to the "weeks" of the exercises, no particular order is imposed on the prayers. The prayer of a Jesuit steeped in the piety of the seventeenth century may be set next to one by a social reformer of the twentieth century. The reflections of a heady theologian or an ecclesiastical statesman may follow the thoughts of an ordinary parish priest.

By using the book you will discover your own best way of praying with it. Some of these prayers may speak to you as soon as you read them; others may seem more obscure. If you are patient with them, you will be rewarded with insights that will deepen your own prayer.

Use the prayers you find helpful. Use them to accompany your retreat or use them when your own words fail to express your feelings on a particular trying or joyful day. You may want to reword them in ways that more accurately state your precise feelings. At other times you may want to go back to a prayer that did not at first seem to have anything to say to you. This is particularly important for poetry, which may take repeated readings to reveal fully all it contains. Each of these prayers is the culmination of a lifetime of prayer.

The spirituality Ignatius bequeathed to the church has indeed enflamed the hearts of people from his generation to ours. The words of Jesuits at prayer are reprinted here with the hope that the hearts of all those who pray them will also be set on fire.

MICHAEL HARTER, SJ
THE FEAST OF ST. IGNATIUS OF LOYOLA
JULY 31, 1993

Prayer for the Beginning of a Retreat

Lord Jesus Christ, present here,
we thank you for the glory
    of your resurrection;
we thank you for having called us together here;
we thank you because you praise the Father
  perfectly in us.
We thank you because you, in us,
    are perfect justice toward our brothers
    and sisters;
it is you in us who continually heal our injustice,
  our mistrust, our fear.
We thank you, Lord Jesus,
    for your great glory
and we offer you what we are about to undertake,
everything we think, do, and experience
    during these coming days in your honor
    and because of you.
We also offer you our fatigue this evening,
    because we are a bit tired
    from the various events of this day,
    as on many other days.
We are content, Lord,
    to offer you this fatigue

because it is our daily vesture.
Grant that, weary and tired as we are,
    we may begin this retreat
    in the name of the Father and of the Son
    and of the Holy Spirit. Amen.

—Carlo Maria Martini, SJ

one

Prayers to Accompany the First Week of the Spiritual Exercises

During the "first week" of the exercises St. Ignatius proposes considerations to help us realize how much we are loved by God. As we ponder God's loving goodness, we usually begin to understand that we have not been wholly generous in our response to that goodness, and we are led to confront the sinfulness in our lives with an honesty we have never before allowed ourselves.

As we experience a growing and intense sorrow for our sins, we are consoled because we are opened to the mercy, goodness, and love of God. Ignatius then encourages us to beg for the grace of being free enough to respond to God's will and to live life with a passion and intensity we have seldom imagined possible.

Use the prayers that follow in this section to deepen your understanding of how much God loves you. Let them give you creative approaches to the examination of conscience. Discover honest, heartfelt ways to express sorrow. But most of all, let these prayers help you develop fresh ways of expressing your love for God.

Soul of Christ

Jesus, may all that is you flow into me.

May your body and blood
    be my food and drink.

May your passion and death
    be my strength and life.

Jesus, with you by my side
    enough has been given.

May the shelter I seek
    be the shadow of your cross.

Let me not run from the love
    which you offer,

But hold me safe from the forces of evil.

On each of my dyings
    shed your light and your love.

Keep calling to me until that day comes,

When, with your saints,
I may praise you forever. Amen.

—David L. Fleming, SJ

This and the following prayer are contemporary paraphrases of the Anima Christi—a favorite prayer of St. Ignatius, which he placed at the beginning of his book of Spiritual Exercises. He frequently suggested that the retreatant conclude a prayer period by reciting this prayer.

I Choose to Breathe the Breath of Christ

I choose to breathe the breath of Christ
    that makes all life holy.
I choose to live the flesh of Christ
    that outlasts sin's corrosion and decay.
I choose the blood of Christ
    along my veins and in my heart
    that dizzies me with joy.
I choose the living waters flowing from his side
    to wash clean my own self and the world itself.
I choose the awful agony of Christ
    to charge my senseless sorrows with meaning
    and to make my pain pregnant with power.
I choose you, good Jesus, you know.
I choose you, good Lord;
    count me among the victories
    that you have won in bitter woundedness.
Never number me among those alien to you.
Make me safe from all that seeks to destroy me.
Summon me to come to you.
Stand me solid among angels and saints
    chanting yes to all you have done,
    exulting in all you mean to do forever and ever.

Then for this time, Father of all,
    keep me, from the core of my self,
    choosing Christ in the world.
Amen.

—Joseph Tetlow, SJ

The First Principle and Foundation

The goal of our life is to live with God forever.
God, who loves us, gave us life.
Our own response of love allows God's life
to flow into us without limit.

All the things in this world are gifts of God,
presented to us so that we can know God more
    easily
and make a return of love more readily.

As a result, we appreciate and use all these gifts of
    God
insofar as they help us develop as loving persons.
But if any of these gifts become the center of our
    lives,
they displace God
and so hinder our growth toward our goal.

In everyday life, then, we must hold ourselves in
    balance
before all of these created gifts insofar as we have a
    choice
and are not bound by some obligation.
We should not fix our desires on health or sickness,

wealth or poverty, success or failure, a long life or
  short one.
For everything has the potential of calling forth in
  us
a deeper response to our life in God.

Our only desire and our one choice should be this:
I want and I choose what better leads
to God's deepening his life in me.

—St. Ignatius of Loyola as paraphrased by
  David L. Fleming, SJ

🔥

Behold God beholding you . . . and smiling.
    —Anthony de Mello, SJ

God's Grandeur

The world is charged with the grandeur of God.
　　It will flame out, like shining from shook foil;
　　It gathers to a greatness, like the ooze of oil
Crushed. Why do men then now not reck his rod?
Generations have trod, have trod, have trod;
　　And all is seared with trade; bleared, smeared
　　　　with toil;
　　And wears man's smudge and shares man's
　　　　smell: the soil
Is bare now, nor can foot feel, being shod.

And for all this, nature is never spent;
　　There lives the dearest freshness deep down
　　　　things;
And though the last lights off the black West went
　　Oh, morning, at the brown brink eastward,
　　　　springs—
Because the Holy Ghost over the bent
　　World broods with warm breast and with ah!
　　　　bright wings.

—Gerard Manley Hopkins, SJ

My Help, My Hope / Psalm 121

I lift my eyes to you
my help, my hope

the heavens (who could imagine?)
the earth (only our Lord)
the infinite starry spaces
the world's teeming breadth

All this. I lift my eyes
—upstart, delighted—
and I praise.

—Daniel Berrigan, SJ

You / Psalm 90

Before ever the mountains arose
[blind from birth they were, mute, dumb]
  You. Are.

  Before the seas
  before the first dawn
  You.
From dust to dust the human story
a crooked line, quickly effaced

  You endure
  You summon
Come; mere sunstruck motes
[Adam stands there, Eve radiant there]

  then
  their course run—
  again
  "Come"
They wither like grass, the perfect and proud.
Words die, suns set, grass blows, a dust.

What then? we must learn
time and again
like infants, on hands and knees
spasmodic wisdom. Six months, sixty years

all one
one blind tug,
at the empyrean. Teach us to count our days
multiple, scanty, no matter. But a voice of praise.

—DANIEL BERRIGAN, SJ

Prayers for the Start of the Day

The Traditional Morning Offering

O Jesus, through the Immaculate Heart of Mary,

I offer you my prayers, works, joys, sufferings of
 this day

in union with the Holy Sacrifice of the Mass
 throughout the world.

I offer them for all the intentions of your Sacred
 Heart:

 the salvation of souls, reparation for sin,
 the reunion of all Christians;

I offer them for the intentions of our bishops,
 and of all Apostles of Prayer, and in particular
 for those recommended by our Holy Father this
 month.

—FROM THE MONTHLY LEAFLET OF THE
APOSTLESHIP OF PRAYER

*The Apostleship of Prayer was founded to promote the devotion to
the Sacred Heart of Jesus. Its members begin each day reciting this
brief prayer consecrating the entire day to the glory of God.*

You Have Called Me by Name

Oh, Lord my God,
You called me from the sleep of nothingness
merely because in your tremendous love
you want to make good and beautiful beings.
You have called me by my name in my mother's
    womb.
You have given me breath and light and movement
and walked with me every moment of my existence.
I am amazed, Lord God of the universe,
that you attend to me and, more, cherish me.
Create in me the faithfulness that moves you,
and I will trust you and yearn for you all my days.

Amen.

—JOSEPH TETLOW, SJ

A Morning Offering

O Jesus, I come before you
at the beginning of this day.

I gaze at your face,
I look upon your side
pierced by the lance.

Your wounded heart speaks to me
of God's love poured out for us.

Take, Lord, and receive my heart:
the words of faith that I speak,
the works of justice I would do,
my joys and sufferings.

~~When I come to the Eucharistic table,~~
Take ~~gather~~ my offerings to your own
for the life of the world.

At the end of the day,
~~place me with Mary, your mother,~~
~~and for her sake~~ take me to your heart. Amen.

*This particular version of the morning offering was circulated on
a vocation-promotion card published by the Maryland Province
Jesuits.*

A Prayer for Spiritual Freedom

O Spirit of God, ~~we~~ *I* ask you to help orient
all my ~~all our~~ actions by your inspirations,
carry them on by your gracious assistance,
May ~~that~~ every prayer and work of ~~ours~~ *mine*
~~may~~ always begin from you
and through you be happily ended.

This prayer is frequently used by Jesuits to begin classes and meetings.

God of My Life

Only in love can I find you, my God.
In love the gates of my soul spring open,
>   allowing me to breathe a new air of freedom
>   and forget my own petty self.
In love my whole being streams forth
>   out of the rigid confines of narrowness and
>   anxious self-assertion,
>   which makes me a prisoner of my own poverty
>   and emptiness.
In love all the powers of my soul flow out toward
you,
>   wanting never more to return,
>   but to lose themselves completely in you,
>   since by your love you are the inmost center of
>   my heart,
>   closer to me than I am to myself.

But when I love you,
when I manage to break out of the narrow circle of
self
and leave behind the restless agony of unanswered
questions,

when my blinded eyes no longer look merely from
    afar
and from the outside upon your unapproachable
    brightness,
and much more when you yourself, O
    Incomprehensible One,
have become through love the inmost center of my
    life,
then I can bury myself entirely in you, O mysterious
    God,
and with myself all my questions.

—KARL RAHNER, SJ

Jesus, Join My Life to Yours

I want to unite my life to your life,
my thoughts to your thoughts,
my affections to your affections,
my heart to your heart,
my works to your works,
my whole self to your self,
in order to become through this union
more holy and more pleasing in the sight of your
   Father
and in order to make my life
more worthy of your grace
and of the reward of eternity.

I want to join your intentions to my intentions,
the holiness of your actions to mine,
and the excellence of your lofty virtues
to the lowliness of mine.

For example, when I pray,
I will join the holiness of your prayer to mine:
in the totality of my life as well as in its every detail,
I will join the whole breadth and height
   of your divine intentions

to whatever I have to do or to suffer.
I will join, if possible, your looks to my eyes,
your holy words to my tongue,
your meekness to my gentleness,
your humiliations and self-emptying to my
    humility,
in a word, your whole divine spirit to my actions:
and when, in some one of my works,
I discover something not inspired by your spirit
and which proceeds rather from my self-
    centeredness
or from some poorly mortified affection,
I will renounce it and disown it with my whole
    heart.
No, my Jesus, I promise myself to have nothing in
    me
    which is not in union with your lofty virtues.

—JEAN-PIERRE MÉDAILLE, SJ

Examination of Conscience

"How do things stand between me and God? Where am I coming from, and where is my life in Christ growing?" I can answer such questions satisfactorily only if I take leisure to reflect. Here is a way of examining this deep and dynamic personal relationship.

- I take time to thank God for the good things that came into my day. I review the many details of the day in no particular order. For instance, I thank God for sunshine or rain, for getting a chair fixed, for a phone call from a friend, for feeling good all day long, for having the energy to get a job done late in the evening. In this process, I may well come across some action that I did or some emotion or desire that I entertained for which I cannot thank God, since it was offensive or sinful.

- Having thanked God for all the day's gifts as much as I can, I beg for this further gift: to see clearly and in hope how I am growing more fully alive to God in them and through them.

- I then examine carefully what my actions, omissions, thoughts, desires tell me about my relationship with God and with myself and others in God. Sometimes, a single event stands out dramatically. For instance: I lost my temper badly; I felt very great joy at a piece of news; I resisted making a decision someone asked me to make; I spent much too long a time on a simple task.

· Patiently, I ask myself what my action or my attitude meant. Did it embody love of God, or fear or distrust? Did it suggest that I have gotten overcommitted, and why would I get overcommitted? Did it suggest that I do not approve of my life or the context in which I live?

· At other times, no event stands out, but I might find a pattern emerging in the day; for instance: all day long I felt anxious and worried; every time I saw a certain person, I wanted to have his or her attention; I got things done swiftly and easily; I erupted in anger over little things. Patiently, I ask myself what a pattern means about my belief in God, and my trust of and love for God.

· At still other times, the climate of my life might emerge as clearly as the day's weather. For instance: I have grown very dissatisfied in my work; I am shaking off an old resentment at something my spouse did; I am deepening in my awareness of God's loving gaze on me; I felt confident all day while asking God for something I want a lot. Patiently again, I ask what this climate shows about me and God.

- Then, I take what I have learned to prayer, speaking to God and telling God whatever I need to say. I let God surprise me with insight and console me with faith and hope. I bring to God the larger needs that I feel right now: an old resentment that I seem unable to shake; an inveterate habit that I badly want to get rid of; a kind of mindless living through the day without thanking and praising my Creator. I beg God to teach me and help me accept the teaching.

- Finally, I determine to keep my spirit filled with gratitude and to take steps to get rid of mind-sets that stand between me and my Creator. I set myself to change an attitude, shake off a fear, or grow in some special way. And I offer this larger movement in my life to God my Creator. I set my mind to accept any other change or shift in my person and myself that would come, were God to give me the larger gift I ask for. God is the Master of my life and myself; I place my trust there, and not in myself.

—Adapted from Joseph Tetlow, SJ

St. Ignatius of Loyola considered this kind of examination perhaps the most important single spiritual exercise we do. His experience brought him to do it daily and to urge all his friends to do the same. This particular explanation of the examination has been adapted from Joseph Tetlow's "Choosing Christ in the World."

A Testament

The following guided meditation is a creative alternative to examining one's conscience. This reflection was proposed by Anthony de Mello, a Jesuit from India who conducted countless workshops throughout the world on the subject of prayer and reflective living.

I imagine that today I am to die.
I ask for time to be alone and write down for my
    friends
a sort of testament for which the points that follow
could serve as chapter titles.

1. These things I have loved in life:
    Things I tasted,
    looked at,
    smelled,
    heard,
    touched.

2. These experiences I have cherished:

3. These ideas have brought me liberation:

4. These beliefs I have outgrown:

5. These convictions I have lived by:

6. These are the things I have lived for:

7. These insights I have gained in the school of life:
   insights into God,
   the world,
   human nature,
   Jesus Christ,
   love,
   religion,
   prayer.

8. These risks I took,
   these dangers I have courted:

9. These sufferings have seasoned me:

10. These lessons life has taught me:

11. These influences have shaped my life
    (persons, occupations, books, events):

12. These Scripture texts have lit my path:

13. These things I regret about my life:

14. These are my life's achievements:

15. These persons are enshrined within my heart:

16. These are my unfulfilled desires:

I choose an ending for this document:

> a poem—my own or someone else's;
> or a prayer;
> a sketch or a picture from a magazine;
> a Scripture text;
> or anything that I judge would be
> an apt conclusion to my testament.

—ANTHONY DE MELLO, SJ

Both what you run away from—and yearn for—is within you.

—ANTHONY DE MELLO, SJ

An Examination of My Use of Time

Killing Time

How do I kill time?
Let me count the ways.

By worrying about things
over which I have no control.
Like the past.
Like the future.

By harboring resentment
and anger
over hurts
real or imagined.

By disdaining the ordinary
or, rather, what I
so mindlessly
call ordinary.

By concern over what's in it for me,
rather than what's in me
for it.

By failing to appreciate what is
because of might-have-beens,
should-have-beens,
could-have-beens.

These are some of the ways
I kill time.

Jesus didn't kill time.
He gave life to it.
His own.

—Leo Rock, SJ

Teach Me to Listen

Teach me to listen, O God,
to those nearest me,
my family, my friends, my co-workers.
Help me to be aware that
no matter what words I hear,
the message is,
"Accept the person I am. Listen to me."

Teach me to listen, my caring God,
to those far from me—
the whisper of the hopeless,
the plea of the forgotten,
the cry of the anguished.

Teach me to listen, O God my Mother,
to myself.
Help me to be less afraid
to trust the voice inside—
in the deepest part of me.

Teach me to listen, Holy Spirit,
for your voice—
in busyness and in boredom,

in certainty and in doubt,
in noise and in silence.

Teach me, Lord, to listen. Amen.

—ADAPTED BY JOHN VELTRI, SJ

Prayers That Express Sorrow

An Act of Contrition

My God, I love you above all things
and I hate and detest with my whole soul
the sins by which I have offended you,
because they are displeasing in your sight,
who are supremely good and worthy to be loved.
I acknowledge that I should love you
with a love beyond all others,
and that I should try to prove this love to you.
I consider you in my mind as infinitely greater
than everything in the world,
no matter how precious or beautiful.
I therefore firmly and irrevocably resolve
never to consent to offend you
or do anything that may displease your sovereign
    goodness
and place me in danger of falling from your holy
    grace,
in which I am fully determined
to persevere to my dying breath. Amen.

—St. Francis Xavier, SJ

Prayer for Light and Help

Jesus, I feel within me
a great desire to please you
but, at the same time,
I feel totally incapable of doing this
without your special light and help,
which I can expect only from you.
Accomplish your will within me—
even in spite of me.

—St. Claude La Colombière, SJ

Prayer for the Grace to Name My Sins

Almighty and all-merciful God,
give me the strength of spirit to name my sins
and the courage to feel shame for them.
Let me feel confounded that my sins
have not destroyed me as others' have.
Teach me to weep for the hurt and harm
I have sinfully inflicted on others.
Please, Lord, I really want to live aware
of how I have let this terrible evil
root itself in my self and in my life world.

—Joseph Tetlow, SJ

A Colloquy with Jesus

At the end, I turn to Jesus Christ, hanging on his
   cross,
and I talk with him.

I ask how can it be that the Lord and Creator
should have come from the infinite reaches of
   eternity
to this death here on earth, so that he could die for
   our sins.

And then I reflect upon myself, and ask:

What have I done for Christ?

What am I doing for Christ?

What ought I do for Christ?

And I talk with Jesus like a friend.

I end with the Our Father.

—Joseph Tetlow, SJ

*In the Spiritual Exercises Ignatius suggests that the retreatant end
each of the meditations on sin with such a conversation.*

Wash Me with Your Precious Blood

See, O merciful God, what return
I, your thankless servant, have made
for the innumerable favors
and the wonderful love you have shown me!
What wrongs I have done, what good left undone!
Wash away, I beg you, these faults and stains
with your precious blood, most kind Redeemer,
and make up for my poverty by applying your
    merits.
Give me the protection I need to amend my life.
I give and surrender myself wholly to you,
and offer you all I possess,
with the prayer that you bestow your grace on me,
so that I may be able to devote and employ
all the thinking power of my mind
and the strength of my body in your holy service,
who are God blessed for ever and ever. Amen.

—St. Peter Canisius, SJ

A Bold Request

I pray, O Master,
that the flames of hell
may not touch me
or any of those whom I love,
and even that they may never touch anyone.
(And I know, my God,
that you will forgive this bold prayer.)

—PIERRE TEILHARD DE CHARDIN, SJ

Prayer for Detachment

I beg of you, my Lord,
to remove anything which separates
me from you, and you from me.

Remove anything that makes me unworthy
of your sight, your control, your reprehension;
of your speech and conversation,
of your benevolence and love.

Cast from me every evil
that stands in the way of my seeing you,
hearing, tasting, savoring, and touching you;
fearing and being mindful of you;
knowing, trusting, loving, and possessing you;
being conscious of your presence

and, as far as may be, enjoying you.
This is what I ask for myself
and earnestly desire from you. Amen.

—BLESSED PETER FABER, SJ

Prayer for Humility

Let me have too deep a sense of humor ever to be
   proud.
Let me know my absurdity before I act absurdly.
Let me realize that when I am humble I am most
   human,
      most truthful,
      and most worthy of your serious
         consideration.

—DANIEL A. LORD, SJ

Forgiving God?

Lord, help me find it in my heart
to forgive you
for making me the way I am.
Blasphemy? Perhaps.
Honesty? For lack of a better word, yes.
In this one repeated blinding
moment of clarity
I honestly need to forgive you, Lord.
I know I am the work of your hands.
I have experienced your gentle touch
in summer breezes
and the warmth of winter fires.
I meet your love in many ways.
In the emptiness of silence
and plentitude of sound;
In light-some revelations
of colorful, moving, living things;
In dead dark night
and still-filled noises;
In thoughts that soar
and feelings that pound;
In good times, bad times, high and lows,
sleeping, waking, seasonally, annually,

every way, everywhere,
each second past,
life-filled full
momentous day,
I am surrounded by your love.

Is it madness, then,
or simply blindness
that keeps me so shortsighted?
Perhaps a bit of both impairs my vision
and will not let the good outside
be seen within.
What reason, traitor? Treason!
I cannot see.
I do not know.
So many things I cannot see.
So many things I do not know.

I have been told you made me
like yourself.
Why then do we two
think so differently?
You made me what I am, Lord.
There is so much I cannot understand,
so much I cannot thank you for.

You who first shared love with me
and showed me how to live;
You whose heart is poured out in creation
and found in forgiveness;
Teach me to forgive your constant
kindnesses to me.

—MICHAEL MOYNAHAN, SJ

A Prayer of Reconciliation

Lord Christ, help us to see what it is
that joins us together, not what separates us.
For when we see only what it is that makes us
    different,
we too often become aware of what is wrong with
    others.
We see only their faults and weaknesses,
interpreting their actions as flowing from
malice or hatred rather than fear.
Even when confronted with evil, Lord,
you forgave and sacrificed yourself
rather than sought revenge.
Teach us to do the same by the power of your Spirit.

—WILLIAM BREAULT, SJ

"I am not worthy to have you come under my roof."(Matthew 8:8)

Lord Christ,
I wish I could offer you
a reasonably clean
and swept house
to dwell in,
but I can't.

I can say—and know the meaning of— "I am not
    worthy to have you come under my roof. . . ."
But you are already there!
Living among the once-flourishing idols.
The floor is dirty
and at times the room is airless—
even for me!
I am ashamed of your presence there,
yet you slept in a cave
and on a donkey's back at night
under the desert stars.
So, if I can't change your accommodations,
let me rejoice all the same
that you are present.
I must believe strongly, Lord,
that I can't question this:

that you are at home
with sinners—
and my greatest sin, Lord Christ,
is that I don't want to be a sinner!
Nor do I easily accept it—still,
    the evidence
    is overwhelming.
But hope is like a green shoot
in the midst of an airless, disordered world.
And that hope comes from your Spirit.
I rest in that hope, Lord.

—WILLIAM BREAULT, SJ

May I Be Worthy of Your Trust

For some strange reason, Lord, you depend upon
   me.
What possible need could you have for my
   shoulder?
Why should you lean on me? Yet you do just that.

I am grateful. It is a challenge and a trust,
an inspiration and a call to character.

If you are willing to depend upon me,
weak and clumsy as I am,
I am eager not to fail you.

Lean on me, dear Lord.
At least pretend to find me a help.
May your sweet pretense
make me worthy of your very real trust.

—Daniel A. Lord, SJ

This prayer is from a series of prayerful reflections Daniel Lord made after he had been diagnosed with cancer.

The Inmost Fear

Why do I fear?
God is here,
deep within—
covering nakedness,
mothering boldness,
sustaining exuberance,
restraining insolence,
siring insight,
firing lovelight,
fulfilling hollowness,
instilling hallowedness
of lung, limb, and life
with tongued fire and crossed strife—
through Christ's indwelling,
outwelling, sorrow-quelling,
joy-swelling victory—
warm love straining
to be heard, to be loved,
yet quiet as a craning ear in silent expectation,
as simple and lonely as a man's sigh,
as rich and crowded as God's sea
in which I swim to eternity
alone in crowded company—
I, a mere glint of God's light,

a mere hint of his might,
yet having the mint of his Son on my heart:
a cross sweeping to God's glorying
and a love flaming with God's worrying—
Christ about me,
in me,
with me,
today the darkening fierce joy of God's sorrow
and then the tranquil swift dawn of God's
  tomorrow.

Why, then, do I fear?
God is here,

        deep within,
        forever:
        Life grandly vibrant,
        Love scandalously flagrant,
        yet heart quietly homing
        and Lord wisely lording.

        But, then,—why do I fear?
        . . . fear . . . fear . . . fear . . .

—David J. Hassel, SJ

Act of Hope and Confidence in God

My God, I believe most firmly
that you watch over all who hope in you,
and that we can want for nothing
when we rely upon you in all things.
Therefore I am resolved for the future . . .
to cast all my cares upon you. . . .

People may deprive me of worldly goods and status.
Sickness may take from me my strength and the
    means of serving you.
I may even jeopardize our relationship by sin,
but my trust shall never leave me.
I will preserve it to the last moment of my life,
and the powers of hell shall seek in vain to grab it
    from me.

Let others seek happiness in their wealth and in
    their talents.
Let them trust in the purity of their lives,
the severity of their mortifications,
in the number of their good works,
the enthusiasm of their prayers,
as for me, my Rock and my Refuge,
my confidence in you fills me with hope.

For you, my Divine Protector, alone have settled me
   in hope.

   "This confidence can never be vain.
   No one, who has hoped in God,
   has ever been confounded."

I am assured, therefore, of my eternal happiness,
for I firmly hope in it and all my hope is in you.

   "In you, O loving God, have I hoped:
   let me never be confounded."

I know too well that I am weak and changeable.
I know the power of temptation against the
   strongest virtue.
I have seen stars fall and foundations of my world
   crack;
these things do not alarm me.
While I hope in you, I am sheltered from all
   misfortune,
and I am sure that my trust shall endure,
for I rely upon you to sustain this unfailing hope.

Finally, I know that my confidence cannot exceed
   your generosity,

and that I shall never receive less than I have hoped
    for from you.
Therefore I hope that you will sustain me against
    my evil inclinations,
that you will protect me
against the deceitful attacks of the evil one,
and that you will cause my weakness

to triumph over every hostile force.
I hope that you will never cease to love me
and that I shall love you unceasingly.

> "In you, O loving God, have I hoped:
> let me never be confounded."

—St. Claude La Colombière, SJ

Scripture Passages for First Week

Luke 11:1–13   "Teach us to pray."

1 Samuel 3:1–10   "Speak, Lord. I want to listen."

Psalm 139   "Lord you search me and you know me."

Jeremiah 29:11–14   "The plans I have are for your welfare."

Isaiah 43   "You are precious in my sight."

Ephesians 2:10   You are God's handiwork.

Mark 10:46–52   "What do you want, Bartimaeus?"

John 5:1–9   "Do you want to be healed?"

Luke 7:36–50   Jesus forgives woman washing his feet.

Seedlings

If any of the short sentences that follow appeals to
you, place it in your heart and ponder on its inner
  meaning.
This will cause its inner truth to germinate and
  grow.

Do not force it open with your mind.
That would only kill the seed.

Sow it where the soil is rich. Sow it in your heart.
And give it time.

> You do not
> have
> to change
> for God
> to love
> you.

> Be grateful
> for your sins.
> They are carriers
> of grace.

Say good-bye
to golden yesterdays
—or your heart
will never learn
to love
the present.

—ANTHONY DE MELLO, SJ

Broken Record

Grandparenting God,
you see our sin as
symptomatic stutter,
self-effacing struggle
to ignore
the confounding reality
of your willful
vulnerability:
"I love you
because I can't do
anything else.
I made you,
every last part of you:
all that's hidden
and all that's revealed,
all that's muddled
and even all that's clear.
You are,
at the risk
of repeating myself,
dear to me.
You are precious
in my eyes

because . . .
just because
you are mine.
That's enough for me.
And it will have to do
for you.

Wrestle with it
until you get tired
and then relax
and give in.
Take a deep breath
and enjoy."

—MICHAEL MOYNAHAN, SJ

An Awareness Examen at the End of the Day

Ask for the light of the Holy Spirit to see through God's eyes . . .

1. What gifts I have received during the day that I can be thankful for.

2. Where God has been working during the day in my life; where I am cooperating with God today; where I am cooperating with the sinful element within me and not doing what I want to do in the Lord (Rom. 7:15–20).

3. The forgiveness God offers for the times when I have not been attentive and responsive to God's presence and love in my life.

4. How God's help will guide me through tomorrow, and that God's Spirit will be with me.

—JOHN VELTRI, SJ (ADAPTED)

Prayer for Generosity

Eternal Word, only begotten Son of God,
Teach me true generosity.
Teach me to serve you as you deserve,
To give without counting the cost,
To fight heedless of wounds,
To labor without seeking rest,
To sacrifice myself without thought of any reward
Save the knowledge that I have done your will.
    Amen.

—ATTRIBUTED TO ST. IGNATIUS OF LOYOLA

TWO

Prayers to Accompany the Second Week of the Spiritual Exercises

For Ignatius, contemplation is natural and spontaneous. In the "second week" of the exercises he invites us to learn and savor this method of prayer. Contemplation and repetition are key aspects of this part of the exercises.

Once we have completed the first week of the exercises, Ignatius invites us to begin contemplating the life of Jesus. He progressively introduces the mysteries of the life of Christ to us. We contemplate Jesus at the very moment of his incarnation, and then we move through the Nativity, hidden life, his baptism in the Jordan, and other appropriate moments in his public ministry.

The Ignatian form of contemplation is alluringly simple. We simply watch as a scene from Scripture unfolds. As we get caught up in the passage, we move beyond being observers and become participants. We hear the words come alive and we actively respond in our own unique ways.

Our emphasis should not be on the quantity of material covered, but on the depth of its assimilation. Ignatius prefers to have us return to a particular scene several times until an entire event in the life of Jesus is distilled into a single phrase or an aspiration that can be carried easily in our hearts.

Practice the method of using Scripture for prayer as outlined on pages 66–71. Pray by reading meditatively examples of how some Jesuits have contemplated the Scriptures. Ponder the poetry. Discover new ways of conversing with Jesus as an intimate friend.

The Windhover

To Christ Our Lord

I caught this morning morning's minion, kingdom of daylight's dauphin, dapple-dawn-
   drawn Falcon, in his riding
  Of the rolling level underneath him steady air,
   and striding
High there, how he rung upon the rein of a
 wimpling wing
In his ecstasy! then off, off forth on swing,
  As a skate's heel sweeps smooth on a bow-
   bend; the hurl and gliding
  Rebuffed the big wind. My heart in hiding
Stirred for a bird,—the achieve of, the mastery of
 the thing!

Brute beauty and valour and act, oh, air, pride,
 plume here
  Buckle! AND the fire that breaks from thee then,
   a billion
Times told lovelier, more dangerous, O my
 chevalier!

No wonder of it: sheer plod makes plough down
    sillion
Shine, and blue-bleak embers, ah my dear,
    Fall, gall themselves, and gash gold-vermilion.

—GERARD MANLEY HOPKINS, SJ

The powerful and majestic images in this poem are taken from nature and are intended by Hopkins to be a tribute to Christ the King. St. Ignatius begins the "second week" of his Spiritual Exercises with a contemplation on Christ as King.

Prayer for What I Want

Lord, grant that I may see thee more clearly,
love thee more dearly,
follow thee more nearly.

—SPIRITUAL EXERCISES §104

Eternal Lord of All Things

Eternal Lord of all things,
I feel your gaze on me.
I sense that your Mother stands near, watching,
and that with you are all the great beings of
   heaven—
angels and powers and martyrs and saints.
Lord Jesus, I think you have put a desire in me.
If you will help me, please,
I would like to make my offering:
I want it to be my desire, and my choice,
provided that you want it, too,
to live my life as you lived yours.
I know that you lived an insignificant person
in a little, despised town;
I know that you rarely tasted luxury and never
   privilege,
and that you resolutely refused to accept power.
I know that you suffered rejection by leaders,
abandonment by friends, and failure.
I know. I can hardly bear the thought of it all.
But it seems a toweringly wonderful thing
that you might call me to follow you and stand with
   you.

I will labor with you to bring God's reign,
if you will give me the gift to do it. Amen.

—Joseph Tetlow, SJ

This prayer is a paraphrase of the colloquy of the meditation on Christ the King, which is placed at the beginning of the second week of the exercises.

🔥

"Viva Cristo Rey —Long Live Christ the King!"
—Blessed Miguel Augustín Pro, SJ

Miguel Pro said this prayer as he extended his arms in the form of a cross and was executed by a firing squad on November 23, 1927, in Mexico for being a priest.

Praying with the Scriptures

God Speaks to Us First

The fundamental truth that God is concerned for each of us long before we became concerned for ourselves makes it possible for us to pray to God. God desires communication with us and speaks to us continually:

- through Jesus Christ, God's Word made flesh;

- through the church, the people who are the extension of Christ in the world;

- through visible creation, another form of God's self-revelation, which is the physical context of our lives;

- through the events and experiences of our lives;

- through Holy Scripture, which is the mode of communication we are most concerned with in prayer.

God Invites Us to Listen

Our response to God's initial move is to listen. This is the basic attitude of prayer.

How to Go About Listening

What you do immediately before prayer is important. Normally, prayer is something you do not rush right into.

Spend a few moments quieting yourself and relaxing, settling into a comfortable, prayerful position.

When listening to anyone, you try to tune out everything except what the person is saying to you. In prayer this can be done best in silence and solitude.

Try to find a quiet place where you can be alone and uninhibited in your response to God's presence. Try to quiet yourself interiorly. In an age of noise, activity, and tensions like our own, it is not always easy or necessary to forget our cares and commitments. Never feel constrained to blot out all distractions. Anxiety in this regard could get between ourselves and God.

Rather, realize that the Word did become flesh and can speak to us in the noise and confusion of our day. Sometimes in preparing for prayer, relax and listen to the sounds around you. God's presence is as real as they are.

Be conscious of your sensations and experiences of feeling, thinking, hoping, loving, wondering, desiring, etc. Then, conscious of God's unselfish, loving presence in you, address God simply: "Yes, you do love life and feeling into me. You are present to me. You live in me. Yes, you do." Then ask for the grace to listen to what God says.

Conversation with God Using Scripture

Select a short passage from Holy Scripture. As you open the book, be aware that you are in the presence of the Living

Word, the One who guarantees all that is written. Read through the passage slowly and attentively; read aloud or whisper in a rhythm with your breathing—a phrase at a time—with pauses and repetitions when and where you feel like it. Do not hurry to cover much material.

If the passage recounts an event in the life of Jesus, enter into the scene as one of the participants. Speak with the persons involved: the blind man being cured or the disciples as they walk with Jesus. Share their attitudes. Respond to what Jesus is saying.

Some words or phrases may carry special meaning for you. Savor those words, repeating them out loud, turning them over in your heart. Think about each of the words or phrases. Who said it? What does it mean? To whom was the word or phrase addressed? What was the speaker feeling?

When something strikes you, pause. Pause, for example, when

- you experience new meaning or a new way of being with Christ (for example, you sense what it means to be healed by Jesus)

- you experience God's love

- you are moved to do something good

- you are peaceful

- you are happy and content just to be in the presence of God

- you are struggling with or disturbed by what the words are saying

This is God speaking directly to you in the words of Scripture. Do not hurry to move on. Wait until you are no longer moved by the experience.

Don't get discouraged if nothing seems to be happening. Sometimes God lets us feel dry and empty in order to let us realize it is not in our own power to experience consolation. God is sometimes very close to us in such a seeming absence (Psalm 139:7–8). God accepts us as we are, with all our limitations—even with our seeming inability to pray. A humble attitude of listening is a sign of love for God and a real prayer from the heart. At these times remember the words of St. Paul: "The Spirit, too, comes to help us in our weakness, for when we cannot choose words in order to pray properly, the Spirit himself expresses our plea in a way that could never be put into words" (Romans 8:26–27).

Relax. Remember, God will speak to you in God's own way. "Yes, as the rain and snow come down from the heavens and do not return without watering the earth, making it yield and giving growth to provide seed for the sower and bread for the eating, so the word that goes from my mouth does not return to me empty, without carrying out my will and succeeding in what it was sent to do" (Isaiah 55:10–11).

Spend time in your prayer just being conscious of God's presence in and around you. If you want to, speak with God about the things you are interested in or wish to be thankful for—your joys, sorrows, aspirations, etc. All along, or as you are coming to the end, think about what this all means to you: to your personal history, your world, your life, your self.

Summary: 6 "P's"

Prepare a Passage from Scripture and have it marked and ready.

Place. Where you are alone and uninhibited in your response to God's presence.

Posture. Relaxed and peaceful. A harmony of body with spirit.

Presence of God. Be aware of it and acknowledge and respond to it. When you are ready, turn to the

Passage. Read the passage from Scripture slowly and listen attentively.

Pause. Don't be anxious. Don't try to look for implications or lessons or profound thoughts or conclusions or resolutions. Be content to be like a child who climbs into its father's or mother's lap and listens to their words and stories.

Carry on a conversation (sometimes called a colloquy) with God about what you have heard. Think of God in the second person singular ("you"). Tell God what you are thinking and feeling. What would you give to God? What do you want of God?

Praying Scripture has nothing to do with "getting through" passages and books; it has everything to do with letting the meaning and the values of each single word sink into your life.

After the period of prayer is over, it may be helpful to reflect back over the experience of prayer. This review will help you notice what the Lord is doing in your experience.

—ARMAND NIGRO, SJ (ADAPTED)

Lord, show me your ways.
　　　—ST. ALPHONSUS RODRIGUEZ, SJ

Scripture Passages for Second Week

The Incarnation and Early Life of Jesus

Luke 1:26–38	Annunciation
Luke 2:1–20	Nativity
Matthew 2:1–12	Adoration of Magi
Luke 2:22–38	Presentation in Temple
Luke 2:39–40, 51–52	Hidden life

Jesus' Public Life

Matthew 3:13–17	Baptism: "This is my beloved Son in whom I am well pleased."
Matthew 4:1–11	Temptation in desert
Luke 4:14–22	The Spirit of the Lord is upon me.
Matthew 5:1–12	Beatitudes (Jesus' value system)
John 1:35–42	"Where do you live?" "Come and see."
Mark 1:16–20	"Come follow me."

Luke 18:18–30	Invitation to rich young man
Luke 5:1–11	"Put out into the deep." Miraculous catch of fish
Matthew 8:23–27	Storm on lake: "Peace, be still."
Matthew 16:13–20	"Who do you say I am?"
Mark 5:25–34	"If only I touch him . . ."
Mark 7:31–37	Cure of the deaf man
Luke 5:17–26	Cure of paralytic: "Your sins are forgiven."
John 5:1–18	"Do you want to be made well?" "Pick up your mat and walk."
John 9:1–41	Cure of man born blind
Luke 8:40–56	Invite Jesus into home: "Lord, I am not worthy."
Luke 19:1–10	Zaccheus
Matthew 14:22–33	"Bid me come to you."
Matthew 17:1–9	Transfiguration
John 11:1–44	Raising of Lazarus: "Unbind him, set him free."

John 15:15–17   "I no longer call you
                                 servants."

Add your own favorite Scripture passages here.

1. Feel free to adapt any of the prayers printed in this
    book. Reword them so they match more closely
    what you feel in your heart.
2. Your deepest longings expressed in your own
    words make the best prayer.
3. Distill the prayer you have done with Scripture to
    a single line, if you can. Rephrase that line until it
    expresses exactly what you feel or want to say.
    Quietly repeat that line again and again. (For ex-
    ample: "Teach me to pray." "Unbind me, set me
    free." "You are mine, on you my favor rests.")

Prayer Before Reading Scripture

We praise and thank you
glorious Lord Jesus Christ,
for being present among us and in us.
In us you praise the Father
with the voice of the Spirit,
whom you have given us.
Lord, may this voice of the Spirit
be roused in us
as we listen to the words of Scripture
in a manner that is worthy and fitting,
appropriate to the meaning of the text and
in harmony with what is revealed to us.
Make us ready to recognize
how we can correspond
to the teaching and example proposed to us.
For you are God, living and reigning
for ever and ever. Amen.

—CARLO MARIA MARTINI, SJ

The following two reflections are creative examples of the way one person contemplates Scripture. They can be used as prayerful reflections in themselves or as models to stimulate your own contemplation of these and other Scripture passages.

Incarnation

We tried in so many ways
to communicate our love.
If communication is not
what you say but
what people hear,
then what we said
was warped and wrenched
into distancing prescriptions
that had no heart.

You asked for food.
We sent manna.
You asked for drink.
Water flowed from the rock.
You asked for directions.
Moses brought the law.
And on and on.
Still you grew
more distant,

more deaf,
more blind.
Memories dulled.
Speech slurred.
Dreams dissolved
into wander dust.

And so we did
what families do
when confronted
with calamity.
We drew straws.
Shorty lost.
He came to share
your plight,
your fight,
your night,
and point you
toward tomorrow.

—MICHAEL MOYNAHAN, SJ

In the Out House

It's been a long,
dusty ride.
A steep and winding road
weaves serpentine
up the side of mountains.
They race the sun
with prospects of a new head to tax,
albeit a small one,
an impending certainty.
Sky and mother
are visual proof.

They reach the city
exhausted
but full of hope.
The husband,
mistaken on occasion
for her father,
fails to act his age
and dashes toward
a door about to close.

"Excuse me.
Could you give us a room for the night?
Some place to lay our heads?"

"Can't you read, buster?
We're all filled up."

"I understand.
It's my wife.
She's about to have her first child."

"That's not my problem."

"He's not a problem.
He's a fact
of life."

"Open your ears, buddy,
because I'm only
gonna say this once.
We ain't got no room.
So scram!"

"I understand"
is drowned
by the sound of a
slammed door.

Three times he will try
to find them lodging.

And with each failure
feel less capable
of caring for his wife
and that life within her
wanting out.

"It doesn't look good.
All their rooms are taken."

"Don't worry.
God will provide."

And all the time thinking:
"That's what I'm afraid of.
They're sorry
but they're full.
It's looking bleak."

"God will give us
what we need."
He shakes his head.
She believes this
and it comforts him little.

The third stop
looking like a
distant bleak relation

of the previous two.
Until the owner's wife
spies the young girl wince
from movement she understands
all too well.

"You can have
the place out back.
It isn't much
but it will be a roof
over your heads.
There's fresh hay thrown.
The animals won't bother you
and the child will be warm.
I'll get some rags and water.
Go on now,
the mother
and baby
are waiting."

Silently
the young girl's face
proclaims:

"Magnificent!"

—MICHAEL MOYNAHAN, SJ

Draw Me into Your Friendship

Lord Jesus, from the start
You invite ordinary people to come to where you
   live.
When they come, you welcome them
and call them to labor and rejoice with you.
You are the most beautiful among all men,
and I hardly believe you want me for your friend.
You are powerful, Lord.
Draw me more and more into your friendship
and lead me along the way you took with friends.

—Joseph Tetlow, SJ

A Child My Choice

Let folly praise that fancy loves, I praise and love
that child,
Whose heart no thought, whose tongue no word,
whose hand no deed defiled.
I praise him most, I love him best, all praise and
love is his;
While him I love, in him I live, and cannot live
amiss.

Love's sweetest mark, laud's highest theme, man's
most desired light,
To love him life, to leave him death, to live in him
delight.
He mine by gift, I his by debt, thus each to other
due.
First friend he was, best friend he is, all times will
try him true.

Though young, yet wise, though small, yet strong;
though man, yet God he is;
As wise he knows, as strong he can, as God he loves
to bless.

His knowledge rules, his strength defends, his love
doth cherish all;
His birth our joy, his life our light, his death our
end of thrall.

Alas! He weeps, he sighs, he pants, yet do his angels
sing;
Out of his tears, his sighs and throbs, doth bud a
joyful spring.
Almighty Babe, whose tender arms can force all
foes to fly,
Correct my faults, protect my life, direct me when I
die.

—St. Robert Southwell, SJ

An Intimate Request

How do you, Lord, look at me?
What do you feel in your heart for me?

—JOHN EAGAN, SJ

Threefold Prayer for Grace to Live Jesus' Values

Ask our Lady to beg Jesus for these gifts for you:
to be received under his standard, and to have the
    courage
to buy into Jesus' value system wholeheartedly.
Ask, if you can, that if God wants it,
you will live a poor and obscure life, the way Jesus
    did,
thought little of by the rich and powerful
as he was thought little of.
(In all this, of course, you would yourself want to do
nothing to offend God, and you would want no one
    else
to do anything that would offend God.)
        End with the "Hail Mary."

Then ask Jesus himself for the privilege of standing
    with him under his standard.
        End by repeating the "Jesus Prayer" for a
        while.*

---

* *The "Jesus Prayer" is simply the words "Lord Jesus Christ, have mercy on me, a sinner" repeated over and over.*

Finally, turn to the Father and ask for these gifts.
End with an Our Father.

—JOSEPH TETLOW, SJ

St. Ignatius suggests making such a prayer at the end of certain key meditations during the second part of the Spiritual Exercises.

Prayer to Know God's Will

May it please the supreme and divine Goodness
to give us all abundant grace
ever to know his most holy will
and perfectly to fulfill it.

—St. Ignatius of Loyola

This prayer was added to the end of many letters St. Ignatius wrote.

Teach Me Your Ways

Teach me your way of looking at people:
as you glanced at Peter after his denial,
as you penetrated the heart of the rich young man
and the hearts of your disciples.

I would like to meet you as you really are,
since your image changes those with whom you
    come into contact.

Remember John the Baptist's first meeting with
    you?
And the centurion's feeling of unworthiness?
And the amazement of all those who saw miracles
    and other wonders?

How you impressed your disciples,
the rabble in the Garden of Olives,
Pilate and his wife
and the centurion at the foot of the cross. . . .

I would like to hear and be impressed
by your manner of speaking,
listening, for example, to your discourse in the
    synagogue in Capharnaum

or the Sermon on the Mount where your audience
felt you "taught as one who has authority."

—Pedro Arrupe, SJ

Help Me Live Your Kingdom

Lord, give me the grace to labor with you
      without seeking myself—
      to live the Kingdom
      in its full reality.

—John Futrell, SJ

Live Eternally in Me

So act, good Jesus,
that, in my relationships with whatever neighbor
and in all I do for the furthering of your Father's
    glory
and the salvation of others,
I form myself on your pattern;
that I be a genuine reflection of your moderation,
gentleness, humility, patience, graciousness,
    tireless zeal,
in a word, of all your virtues;
and, in order to engrave them in my soul,
live eternally in me.

—JEAN-PIERRE MÉDAILLE, SJ

Teach Me Thy Paths

Show, O Lord, Thy ways to me,
and teach me Thy paths.
Direct me in Thy truth, and teach me;
for Thou art God my Saviour.

—BLESSED PETER FABER, SJ

🔥

Lord, let me know you, let me know myself.

Lord, you do your will and not mine.

I'm just coming, Lord.
—ST. ALPHONSUS RODRIGUEZ, SJ

These three brief aspirations are examples of Alphonsus Rodriguez's customary way of praying. For many years this humble laybrother answered the door at the Jesuit college on the Mediterranean island of Majorca, where he tried to see Christ in each of the guests who came to the door. See the poem on page 133 which Gerard Manley Hopkins wrote in his honor.

A Contemporary Annotation

"Much is expected
from those to whom
much has been given." [Luke 12:48]

We have been given the same Word,
graced by the same Spirit
and nourished at the same table as
Oscar Romero, Rutilio Grande,
Ita Ford, Dorothy Kazel,
Jeanne Donovan, and Maura Clark.

—STEPHEN PRIVETT, SJ

Center of Our Hearts

O God, what will you do to conquer
the fearful hardness of our hearts?
Lord, you must give us new hearts,
tender hearts, sensitive hearts,
to replace hearts that are made of marble and of
  bronze.

You must give us your own Heart, Jesus.
Come, lovable Heart of Jesus.
Place your Heart deep in the center of our hearts
and enkindle in each heart a flame of love
as strong, as great, as the sum of all the reasons
that I have for loving you, my God.

O holy Heart of Jesus, dwell hidden in my heart,
so that I may live only in you and only for you,
so that, in the end, I may live with you eternally in
  heaven.
Amen.

—St. Claude La Colombière, SJ

Show Me Your Face, O God / Psalm 61

At land's end, end of tether
   where the sea turns in sleep
      ponderous, menacing
         and my spirit fails and runs
     landward, seaward, askelter

        I pray you
          make new
        this hireling heart
           O
         turn your face to me
       —winged, majestic, angelic—

           tireless,

            a tide

         my prayer goest up—
      show me your face, O God!

—DANIEL BERRIGAN, SJ

Personal Prayer of Pedro Arrupe

Grant me, O Lord, to see everything now with new
 eyes,
to discern and test the spirits
that help me read the signs of the times,
to relish the things that are yours, and to
 communicate them to others.
Give me the clarity of understanding that you gave
 Ignatius.

—PEDRO ARRUPE, SJ

♦

O God, give me the courage and strength to be worthy
of being called a Christian.

—KARL RAHNER, SJ

True Friend

Jesus, you are my true friend, my only friend.
You take a part in all my misfortunes;
You take them on yourself;
You know how to change them into blessings.

You listen to me with the greatest kindness
when I relate my troubles to you,
and you always have balm to pour on my wounds.
I find you at all times, I find you everywhere,
You never go away;
if I have to change my dwelling, I find you wherever
    I go.
You are never weary of listening to me,
You are never tired of doing me good.
I am certain of being beloved by you if I love you;
my goods are nothing to you,
and by bestowing yours on me you never grow poor.
However miserable I may be,
no one nobler or wiser or even holier
can come between you and me,
and deprive me of your friendship;
and death, which tears us away from all other
    friends,
will unite me forever to you.

All the humiliations attached to old age
or to the loss of honor will never detach you from
    me.
On the contrary, I shall never enjoy you more fully,
and you will never be closer to me
than when everything seems to conspire against
    me,
to overwhelm me, and to cast me down.
You bear with all my faults with extreme patience,
and even my want of fidelity and ingratitude
do not wound you to such a degree
as to make you unwilling to receive me back
when I return to you.

Jesus, grant that I may die praising you,
that I may die loving you,
that I may die for the love of you. Amen.

—St. Claude La Colombière, SJ

The Face of Christ

The tragic beauty of the face of Christ
shines in the face of man;

the abandoned old live on
in shabby rooms, far from inner comfort.
Outside, in the street
din and purpose, the world like a fiery animal
reined in by youth. Within
a pallid tiring heart
shuffles about its dwelling.

Nothing, or so little, comes of life's promise.
Out of broken men, despised minds
what does one make—
a roadside show, a graveyard of the heart?

The Christian God reproves
faithless ranting minds
crushing like upper and lower stones
all life between;
Christ, fowler of street and hedgerow
of cripples and the distempered old
—eyes blind as woodknots,
tongues tight as immigrants—

takes in his gospel net
all the hue and cry of existence.

Heaven, of such imperfection,
wary, ravaged, wild?

Yes. Compel them in.

—DANIEL BERRIGAN, SJ

Patient Trust

Above all, trust in the slow work of God.
We are quite naturally impatient in everything
        to reach the end without delay.
We should like to skip the intermediate stages.
We are impatient of being on the way to something
        unknown, something new.
And yet it is the law of all progress
        that it is made by passing through
        some stages of instability—
        and that it may take a very long time.

And so I think it is with you;
        your ideas mature gradually—let them grow,
        let them shape themselves, without undue
            haste.
Don't try to force them on,
        as though you could be today what time
        (that is to say, grace and circumstances
        acting on your own good will)
        will make of you tomorrow.

Only God could say what this new spirit
        gradually forming within you will be.

Give our Lord the benefit of believing
    that his hand is leading you,
and accept the anxiety of feeling yourself
    in suspense and incomplete.

—PIERRE TEILHARD DE CHARDIN, SJ

As Kingfishers Catch Fire

As kingfishers catch fire, dragonflies draw flame;
　　As tumbled over rim in roundy wells
　　Stones ring; like each tucked string tells, each
　　　　hung bell's
Bow swung finds tongue to fling out broad its name;
Each mortal thing does one thing and the same;
　　Deals out that being indoors each one dwells;
　　Selves—goes itself; myself it speaks and spells;
Crying What I do is me: for that I came.

I say more: the just man justices;
　　Keeps grace: that keeps all his goings graces;
Acts in God's eye what in God's eye he is—

　　Christ—for Christ plays in ten thousand places,
Lovely in limbs, and lovely in eyes not his
　　To the Father through the features of men's
　　　　faces.

—Gerard Manley Hopkins, SJ

Peace
is only found
in yes.
　　　—Anthony de Mello, SJ

THree

Prayers to Accompany the Third Week of the Spiritual Exercises

Contemplation of the life of Jesus continues during the "third week," but now we focus on the passion and death of Jesus. It is not easy to be with a person who is suffering. But if the person suffering is a close friend or a family member, we cannot allow ourselves to be anyplace other than by his or her side.

As ones who love Jesus and have desired to walk with him, we intensely long to be wherever he is. And so when the one we have grown to love is suffering, then we know we must be right there with him. But desiring to be by Jesus' side (or at the side of our suffering brother or sister) and actually being there are different matters. We may find ourselves tempted to escape from sheer terror, but stay we must.

The grace Ignatius asks the retreatant to pray for during the third week is "sorrow, compassion, and shame because the Lord is going to his suffering for my sins." Even here the focus remains on the Lord. In asking for such a grace, we are not seeking to shoulder a heavy burden of guilt, but to ponder a mystery of love—that Jesus could love us enough to suffer and die for us.

To ponder the Passion is truly a grace. No one lightly chooses it. And how one participates in it is entirely at the discretion of God.

The prayers that follow are written by Jesuits who have been invited to experience the Lord's passion through sickness, suffering, and even martyrdom. Their words can help us take a further step into the mystery of suffering.

A Prayer for Compassion

Oh God, I wish from now on
to be the first to become conscious
of all that the world loves, pursues, and suffers;

I want to be the first to seek,
to sympathize, and to suffer;
the first to unfold and sacrifice myself,

to become more widely human
and more nobly of the earth
than any of the world's servants.

—Pierre Teilhard de Chardin, SJ

Thou art indeed just, Lord

Thou art indeed just, Lord, if I contend
With thee; but, sir, so what I plead is just.
Why do sinners' ways prosper? and why must
Disappointment all I endeavour end?
Wert thou my enemy, O thou my friend,
How wouldst thou worse, I wonder, than thou dost
Defeat, thwart me? Oh, the sots and thralls of lust
Do in spare hours more thrive than I that spend,
Sir, life upon thy cause. See, banks and brakes
Now, leavèd how thick! lacèd they are again
With fretty chervil, look, and fresh wind shakes
Them; birds build—but not I build; no, but strain,
Time's eunuch, and not breed one work that wakes.
Mine, O thou lord of life, send my roots rain.

—GERARD MANLEY HOPKINS, SJ

The Eucharist and Our Daily Lives

Come, Lord, enter my heart,
you who are crucified, who have died, who love,
who are faithful, truthful, patient, and humble,
you who have taken upon yourself a slow and
    toilsome life
in a single corner of the world,
denied by those who are your own,
too little loved by your friends,
betrayed by them, subjected to the law,
made the plaything of politics right from the very
    first,
a refugee child, a carpenter's son, a creature who
    found
only barrenness and futility as a result of his labors,
a man who loved and who found no love in
    response,
you who were too exalted for those about you to
    understand,
you who were left desolate,
who were brought to the point of feeling yourself
    forsaken by God,
you who sacrificed all,
who commend yourself into the hands of your
    Father,

you who cry: "My God, my Father,
            why have you forsaken me?"
I will receive you as you are,
make you the innermost law of my life,
take you as at once the burden and the strength of
    my life.
When I receive you I accept my everyday just as
    it is.
I do not need to have any lofty feelings in my heart
    to recount to you.
I can lay my everyday before you just as it is,
for I receive it from you yourself,
the everyday and its inward light,
the everyday and its meaning,
the everyday and the power to endure it,
the sheer familiarity of it,
which becomes the dimmedness of your eternal
    life.

—Karl Rahner, SJ

Enfold Me in Your Heart

Lord, enfold me in the depths of your heart;
and there hold me, refine, purge, and set me on
   fire,
raise me aloft, until my own self knows utter
   annihilation.

—Pierre Teilhard de Chardin, SJ

I Take My Stand on His Word / Psalm 130

Out of the depths I cry to you, Lord
Lord hear my voice
be attentive to my cry.

If you remember our sin
who could bear it?

No, your glory is your forgiveness.

My soul hopes in the Lord;
I take my stand on his word.

More than the sleepless awaiting the dawn
my soul awaits him.

As a vigiler awaits the dawn
let his friends await the Lord.

For with him is grace in abundance!
Out of the depths
I take my stand on his word.

—DANIEL BERRIGAN, SJ

May Jesus' Death Be My Life

O Christ Jesus,
may your death be my life,
your labor my repose,
your human weakness my strength,
your confusion my glory.

—Blessed Peter Faber, SJ

Perfect Resignation

My God, I do not know what must come to me
    today.
But I am certain that nothing can happen to me
that you have not foreseen, decreed, and ordained
    from all eternity.
That is sufficient for me.
I adore your impenetrable and eternal designs,
to which I submit with all my heart.
I desire, I accept them all, and I unite my sacrifice
to that of Jesus Christ, my divine Savior.
I ask in his name and through his infinite merits,
patience in my trials, and perfect and entire
    submission
to all that comes to me by your good pleasure.
    Amen.

—St. Joseph Pignatelli, SJ

Prayer for Compassion

Teach me how to be compassionate to the suffering,
to the poor, the blind, the lame, and the lepers;

show me how you revealed your deepest emotions,
as when you shed tears,
or when you felt sorrow and anguish
to the point of sweating blood
and needed an angel to console you.

Above all, I want to learn
how you supported the extreme pain of the cross,
including the abandonment of your Father.

—PEDRO ARRUPE, SJ

Prayer for Obtaining Holy Self-Abandonment

O my God, when will it please you
to give me the grace of remaining habitually
in that union of my will with your adorable will,
in which, without our saying anything, all is said,
and in which we do everything by letting you act.
In this perfect union of wills we perform immense
    tasks
because we work more in conformity with your
    good pleasure;
and yet we are dispensed from all toil
because we place the care of everything in your
    hands,
and think of nothing but of reposing completely in
    you—
a delightful state which
even in the absence of all feelings of faith
gives the soul an interior and altogether spiritual
    relish.
Let me say then unceasingly
through the habitual disposition of my heart.
"Fiat! Yes, my God, yes,
everything that you please.

May your holy desires be fulfilled in everything.
I give up my own which are blind,
perverse and corrupted by that miserable self-love
which is the mortal enemy of your grace and pure
    love,
of your glory and my own sanctification."

—Jean-Pierre de Caussade, SJ

There are truths that can only be discovered through
suffering or from the critical vantage point of extreme
situations.

    —Ignacio Martín-Baró, SJ

A Free Oblation of Self

I have made a free oblation of myself
to your Divine Majesty,
both of life and of death,
and I hope that you will give me
grace and force to perform.
This is all I desire. Amen.

—St. Edmund Campion, SJ

In the Hands of God

More than ever I find myself in the hands of God.
This is what I have wanted all my life from my
    youth.

But now there is a difference;
the initiative is entirely with God.

It is indeed a profound spiritual experience
to know and feel myself so totally in God's hands.

—PEDRO ARRUPE, SJ

Pedro Arrupe composed this prayer after he suffered a debilitating stroke, the effects of which he patiently endured for the final ten years of his life.

All That I Have I Give

Lord, I'm not turning back.
All that I have I now give to you.
Ask me whatever;
I never want to betray you.

—Carlo Maria Martini, SJ

An Offering of Self

O Jesus, my life and my glory,
I cheerfully restore the life
which I have received from thee,
and were it not thy gift,
would not be mine to return.

I have ever desired, O God of my soul,
to resign my life to thee and for thee.
The loss of life for thy sake, I own my advantage. . . .

I die for the love of thee.

—St. Edmund Arrowsmith, SJ

A Prayer to Seek the Consolation of the Cross

Jesus, love of my soul, center of my heart!
Why am I not more eager
to endure pains and tribulations for love of you,
when you, my God, have suffered so many for me?

Come, then, every sort of trial in the world,
for this is my delight, to suffer for Jesus.
This is my joy, to follow my Savior,
and to find my consolation
with my consoler on the cross.

This is my happiness, this my pleasure:
to live with Jesus, to walk with Jesus,
to converse with Jesus;
to suffer with and for him,
this is my treasure.

—St. Alphonsus Rodriguez, SJ

A Commendation to the Providence of God

Loving and tender providence of my God,
into your hands I commend my spirit;
to you I abandon my hopes and fears,
my desires and repugnances,
my temporal and eternal prospects.

To you I commit the wants of my perishable body;
to you I commit the more precious interests
   of my immortal soul
for whose lot I have nothing to fear
as long as I do not leave your care.

Though my faults are many, my misery great,
my spiritual poverty extreme,
my hope in you surpasses all.
It is superior to my weakness,
greater than my difficulties,
stronger than death.

Though temptations should assail me,
I will hope in you;
though I break my resolutions,

I will look to you confidently for grace to keep them
    at last.
Though you should ask me to die,
even then I will trust in you,
for you are my Father, my God,
the support of my salvation.

You are my kind, compassionate, and indulgent
    parent,
and I am your devoted son,
who casts myself into your arms and begs your
    blessing.
I put my trust in you,
and so trusting, shall not be confounded. Amen.

—St. Claude La Colombière, SJ

A Prayer Asking to Stand Near Mary

Let me spend my life near thee, O Mother,
to keep thee company in thy solitude and deepest
    grief;
let me feel in my soul the sadness of thine eyes
and the abandonment of thy heart.

On life's highway I do not seek the gladness of
    Bethlehem;
I do not wish to adore the Infant God in thy virginal
    hands,
nor to enjoy the winsome presence of Jesus
in thy humble home of Nazareth,
nor to mingle with the angelic choirs in thy glorious
    Assumption.

My wish in life is for the jeers and derision of
    Calvary;
for the slow agony of thy Son,
for the contempt, the disgrace and infamy of the
    Cross.
My wish, O most sorrowful Virgin, is to stand near
    thee,
to strengthen my soul through thy tears,
to complete my offering through thy martyrdom,

to temper my heart through thy solitude,
and to love my God and thy God through my self-
    sacrifice.

—Blessed Miguel Augustín Pro, SJ

Prayer for New Life through Death to Sin

Through your most holy passion and death,
I beg of you, Lord, to grant me a most holy life,
and a most complete death to all my vices and
    passions and self-love
and to grant me sight of your holy faith, hope, and
    charity.

—St. Alphonsus Rodriguez, SJ

O Deus, Ego Amo Te

O God, I love Thee, I love Thee—
Not out of hope of heaven for me
Nor fearing not to love and be
in the everlasting burning.
Thou, Thou, my Jesus, after me
Didst reach Thine arms out dying,
For my sake sufferedst nails and lance,
Mocked and marred countenance,
Sorrows passing number,
Sweat and care and cumber,
Yea and death, and this for me,
And Thou couldst see me sinning;
Then I, why should not I love Thee,
Jesus, so much in love with me?
Not for heaven's sake; not to be
Out of hell by loving Thee;
Not for any gains I see;
But just the way that Thou didst me
I do love and I will love Thee:
What must I love Thee, Lord, for then?
For being my king and God. Amen.

—Attributed to St. Francis Xavier, SJ

The translation of this prayer is by Gerard Manley Hopkins, SJ.

From Death to Life

Jesus Christ, may your death be my life
and in your dying may I learn how to live.
May your struggles be my rest,
Your human weakness my courage,
Your embarrassment my honor,
Your passion my delight,
Your sadness my joy,
in your humiliation may I be exalted.
In a word, may I find all my blessings in your trials.
  Amen.

—BLESSED PETER FABER, SJ

Scripture Passages for Third Week

Matthew 26:17–27:66	Passion of Christ
Mark 14:10–15:47	Passion of Christ
Luke 22:1–23:56	Passion of Christ
John 18:1–19:42	Passion of Christ
Psalm 22	Why have you forsaken me?
2 Corinthians 5:14–15	The love of Christ overwhelms us.
Ephesians 5:1–2	Love as Jesus loved you.
Galatians 2:19–20	I have been crucified with Christ.
1 John 3:16	He taught us love.

In Honour of St. Alphonsus Rodriguez

Honour is flashed off exploit, so we say;
And those strokes once that gashed flesh or galled
     shield
Should tongue that time now, trumpet now that
     field,
And, on the fighter, forge his glorious day.

On Christ they do and on the martyr may;
But be the war within, the brand we wield
Unseen, the heroic breast not outward-steeled,
Earth hears no hurtle then from fiercest fray.

Yet God (that hews mountain and continent,
Earth, all, out; who, with trickling increment,
Veins violets and tall trees makes more and more)
Could crowd career with conquest while there went
Those years and years by of world without event
That in Majorca Alfonso watched the door.

—Gerard Manley Hopkins, SJ

Entrusting Myself to the Hands of Jesus

I've come to think that the only, the supreme,
    prayer
we can offer up, during these hours
when the road before us is shrouded in darkness,
is that of our Master on the cross:
'In manus tuas commendo spiritum meum.'
To the hands that broke and gave life to the bread,
that blessed and caressed, that were pierced; . . .
to the kindly and mighty hands that reach down
to the very marrow of the soul—that mould and
    create—
to the hands through which so great a love is
    transmitted—
it is to these that it is good to surrender our soul,
above all when we suffer or are afraid.
And in so doing there is a great happiness and great
    merit.

—Pierre Teilhard de Chardin, SJ

Into the Mystery of Jesus' Life and Death

Mary, Mother of Jesus and our Mother,
we place ourselves with you
at the foot of your Son's cross,
asking you to help us enter
into the mystery of his life and death;
to dwell in his heart;
to remain at his feet
in an attitude of listening and contemplation.
Arouse in us, Mary, your sentiments of
    participation
in the suffering of Christ and of the world.

You see how imperfect our words are
and how far removed our concepts are
from the truth that you live.
Help each one of us;
help everyone who is united with our prayer
and our adoration.

Grant us joy in your Son by the Holy Spirit's grace,
   which we implore from the power of the Father.
   Amen.

—CARLO MARIA MARTINI, SJ

In the shadow of death may we not look back to the
past, but seek in utter darkness the dawn of God.
   —PIERRE TEILHARD DE CHARDIN, SJ

A Hollowed Space to Be Filled

A cup must be empty before it can be filled.
If it is already full, it can't be filled again except by
    emptying it out.
In order to fill anything, there must be a hollowed-
    out space.
Otherwise it can't receive.

This is especially true of God's word.
In order to receive it, we must be hollowed out.
We must be capable of receiving it,
emptied of the false self and its endless demands.

When Christ came, there was no room in the inn.
It was full. The inn is a symbol of the heart.
God's word, Christ, can take root only in a hollow.

—WILLIAM BREAULT, SJ

Prayer to Mary to Understand the Cross

Grant, O Lord, that in our contemplation
of the mystery of your passion
we do not run away from the essential things.
Help us to contemplate you,
your eucharistic love,
your crucified love as the sum reality necessary
    to understand all the rest,
    as the one reality from which
    all the others receive light and clarity.

We ask you this through the intercession
of the one who had the eye to see all essential
   things:
Mary, your mother.

—CARLO MARIA MARTINI, SJ

Who Lives in Love

Who lives in love, loves least to live,
and long delays doth rue,

If him he love by whom he lives,
to whom all praise is due,

Who for our love did choose to live,
and was content to die,

Who loved our love more than his life,
and love with life did buy.

Let us in life, yea with our life,
requite his living love,

For best we live when least we live,
if love our life remove.

Mourn therefore no true lover's death,
life only him annoys,

And when he taketh leave of life
then love begins his joys.

—St. Robert Southwell, SJ

🔥

Lord, help me enter into that peace which consists in
having put my life in your hands.

—Carlo Maria Martini, SJ

Repentance reaches fullness when you are brought to
gratitude for your sins.

—Anthony de Mello, SJ

four

Prayers to Accompany the Fourth Week of the Spiritual Exercises

During the final (and briefest) of the weeks of the exercises, Ignatius directs us to enter into the joy of Christ. We have contemplated the total self-oblation of Jesus in his passion during the third week. In the "fourth week" we contemplate Jesus as he shares the joy of his resurrection with his friends. Now we let the reality of his resurrection permeate our own lives.

There is nothing superficial about the joy of the fourth week. It is profoundly realistic because it is set in the context of the entire flow of the exercises. What began in the absolute honesty of the first week grew and matured through our journey with Jesus as we contemplated his public life and passion. Though we are sinners, we are forgiven because we are loved. And as we model our lives on the life of Jesus who died and rose again, so we must be willing to die to our own individual and communal sinfulness as we hope to rise to new life.

Ignatius saves his best for the end. He guides us through what he calls a *contemplatio ad amorem*—an immersion in the reality of a loving God. He invites us to review all we have pondered about how God loves us and to imprint indelibly upon our hearts the truth that God labors through every aspect of creation to love us into life.

In the end we can only stand in awe in the presence of our God who loves us. We pray that as we have come to some small understanding of the way God loves us, we may strive to love God and to manifest that love in the way we relate to our friends and neighbors.

Putting Love into Practice

Love consists in sharing
what one has
and what one is
with those one loves.

Love ought to show itself in deeds
more than in words.

—St. Ignatius of Loyola

What I Want and Desire

I ask the Father to give me an intimate knowledge of the many gifts I have received that filled with gratitude for all, I may in all things love and serve the Divine Majesty.

—SPIRITUAL EXERCISES §233

Glory Glory / Psalm 19

The heavens bespeak the glory of God.
The firmament ablaze, a text of his works.
Dawn whispers to sunset
Dark to dark the word passes; glory glory.

All in a great silence,
no tongue's clamor—
yet the web of the world trembles
conscious, as of great winds passing.

The bridegroom's tent is raised,
a cry goes up: He comes! a radiant sun
rejoicing, presiding, his wedding day.
From end to end of the universe his progress
No creature, no least being but catches fire from
    him.

—Daniel Berrigan, SJ

Hymn to Matter

Blessed be you, harsh matter,
barren soil, stubborn rock;
you who yield only to violence:
you who force us to work if we would eat.

Blessed be you, perilous matter,
violent sea, untameable passion:
you, who unless we fetter you, will devour us.

Blessed be you, mighty matter,
irresistible march of evolution, reality ever
    new-born;
you who by constantly shattering our mental
    categories,
force us to go ever further in our pursuit of truth.

Blessed be you, universal matter,
immeasurable time, boundless other, abyss of
    starts and atoms and generations;
you, who by overflowing and dissolving our narrow
    standards or measurements,
reveal to us the dimensions of God.

I acclaim you as the melodious fountain of water
from whom springs the souls of all people,
and as the limpid crystal,
whereof is fashioned the new Jerusalem.

I acclaim you as the divine milieu,
charged with creative power,
as the ocean stirred by the spirit,
as the clay molded and infused with life by the
    incarnate Word.

Your realm comprises those supreme heights
where saints think to avoid you—
but where your flesh is so transparent and so agile
as to be no longer distinguishable from spirit.

Raise me up then, matter,
to those heights through struggle and separation
    and death;
raise me up until at long last it becomes possible
    for me,
in perfect chastity, to embrace the universe.

—Pierre Teilhard de Chardin, SJ

Praise to the Father

To God, the Father of mercies,
light and source of all good,
Lord of history and of the universe,
goal of the entire human journey,
we lift our praise.
To you, Father, be praise in the church and in the
    world,
in earthly history and in heaven.
May Mary, Mother of Jesus, praise you;
may the angels praise you;
may the thrones and dominions praise you;
may the saints praise you;
may our deceased praise you;
may everyone we meet praise you,
that we all may be able to unite
in a hymn acknowledging the fullness of glory
which your Son communicates to us
in the grace of the Spirit who animates our hearts.
    Amen.

—Carlo Maria Martini, SJ

You sanctify whatever you are grateful for.
    —Anthony de Mello, SJ

My Lord and My God

Glorious Lord Christ:
the divine influence secretly diffused and active
in the depths of matter,
and the dazzling centre
where all the innumerable fibres of the manifold
    meet;
power as implacable as the world and as warm as
    life;
you whose forehead is of the whiteness of snow,
whose eyes are of fire,
and whose feet are brighter than molten gold;
you whose hands imprison the stars;
you who are the first and the last,
the living and the dead and the risen again;
you who gather into your exuberant unity
every mode of existence;
it is you to whom my being cries out
with a desire as vast as the universe:
"In truth you are my Lord and my God."

—Pierre Teilhard de Chardin, SJ

On the day you cease to change you cease to live.
    —Anthony de Mello, SJ

Scripture Passages for Fourth Week

Resurrection Appearances

Mark 16:1–8	"Where have you put him?" "Mary!"
John 20:19–23	"Peace be with you."
Luke 24:13–35	Emmaus. They recognized him in the breaking of the bread.
John 20:24–29	Thomas: "My Lord and my God!"
John 21:1–17	"It is the Lord." "Feed my sheep."
Matthew 28:16–20	Ascension: "Go forth. I am with you always."
Acts 2:1–4	Holy Spirit enflames the disciples.
2 Corinthians 1:3–5	We share abundantly in Christ's consolation.

From the Journal of St. Ignatius

Eternal Father, confirm me;
Eternal Son, confirm me;
Holy Spirit, confirm me;
Holy Trinity, confirm me;
my one only God, confirm me.

—St. Ignatius of Loyola

Help Us to Remain Close to You

Lord Jesus, we ask you now
to help us to remain with you always,
to be close to you with all the ardor of our hearts,
to take up joyfully the mission you entrust to us,
and that is to continue your presence
and spread the good news of your resurrection.

—CARLO MARIA MARTINI, SJ

Father, in the name of Jesus, give me the Spirit.

—BLESSED PETER FABER, SJ

"Seek God in all things and we shall find God by our side."

—ST. PETER CLAVER, SJ

Pied Beauty

Glory be to God for dappled things—
> For skies of couple-colour as a brinded cow;
>> for rose-moles all in stipple upon trout that
>> swim;

Fresh-firecoal chestnut-falls; finches' wings;
> Landscape plotted and pieced—fold, fallow, and
>> plough;
>> And all trades, their gear and tackle and trim.

All things counter, original, spare, strange;
> Whatever is fickle, freckled (who knows how?)
> With swift, slow; sweet, sour; adazzle, dim;
He fathers-forth whose beauty is past change:
>> Praise him.

—Gerard Manley Hopkins, SJ

God Bless the World

Mighty God, Father of all,
Compassionate God, Mother of all,
bless every person I have met,
every face I have seen,
every voice I have heard,
especially those most dear;
bless every city, town, and
street that I have known,
bless every sight I have seen,
every sound I have heard,
every object I have touched.
In some mysterious way these
have all fashioned my life;
all that I am,
I have received.
Great God, bless the world.

—JOHN J. MORRIS, SJ

Suscipe (Traditional)

Take, Lord, and receive all my liberty,
my memory, my understanding,
and my entire will,
all I have and call my own.

You have given all to me.
To you, Lord, I return it.

Everything is yours; do with it what you will.
Give me only your love and your grace,
that is enough for me.

—St. Ignatius of Loyola

Suscipe (Paraphrase)

Accept, O Lord, and treat as your own
my liberty, my understanding,
my memory—all of my decisions and
my freedom to choose.
All that I am and all that I have
you gave and give to start;
now I turn and return all to you,
looking to find your hopes and will in all.
Keep giving me your holy love,
Hold on me your life-giving gaze,
and I neither need nor want anything else.

—Joseph Tetlow, SJ

Extend your arms in welcome to the future. The best is
yet to come!

—Anthony de Mello, SJ

Devotional Materials

Litany of Jesuit Saints

Ignatius Loyola,
>   our holy founder, man of great desires and
>   perfect humility, ... *Pray for us.*

Francis Xavier,
>   courageous warrior ever seeking new souls for
>   Christ, . . .

Peter Faber,
>   first companion of Ignatius and cherished
>   friend of all, . . .

Stanislaus Kostka,
>   of ready heart and single mind, . . .

Francis Borgia,
>   nobleman of poverty, model of
>   indifference, . . .

Edmund Campion,
>   fearless orator and source of courage to the
>   persecuted, . . .

Aloysius Gonzaga,
>   consolation and care for the sick and the
>   dying, . . .

Robert Southwell,
> prisoner-poet of comfort and strength, . . .

Peter Canisius,
> scholar, builder, and teacher of little
> children, . . .

Nicholas Owen,
> clever carpenter, companion loyal to the
> death, . . .

Alphonsus Rodriguez,
> mystical friend, model of hospitality, . . .

Robert Bellarmine,
> rich of mind yet poor of spirit, . . .

John Berchmans,
> single-hearted student, model of
> simplicity, . . .

John Francis Regis,
> compassionate confessor, rekindler of burnt-
> out faith, . . .

Isaac Jogues,
> trusting missionary, obedient unto death, . . .

John de Brébeuf,
> lover of the cross and the name of Jesus, . . .

Peter Claver,
>   tireless lover of the poor and the powerless, . . .

Claude La Colombière,
>   faithful servant and perfect friend of the loving
>   heart of Christ, . . .

Gerard Manley Hopkins,
>   catcher of fire and crafter of words, . . .

Pierre Teilhard de Chardin,
>   mystical lover of all that is and all that is to
>   be, . . .

Rutilio Grande,
>   devoted pastor of the poor and the
>   oppressed, . . .

Karl Rahner,
>   professor of prayer and loyal servant of the
>   church, . . .

Ignacio Ellacuría and companions,
>   fearless and faithful proclaimers of the Good
>   News in the face of persecution, . . .

Pedro Arrupe,
>   grace-filled leader of renewal and
>   rededication, . . .

Concluding Prayer

> Almighty and ever-watchful God,
> Lord of the heavens above and the earth below
>
> Your Divine Goodness created us in love
> from every region of North and Central America:
>
> > from Fond du Lac and Topeka
> > Orange Walk and Dangriga
> > Denver and New Orleans
> > Merida and Arnold
> > St. Louis and Kansas City
>
> Your Divine Wisdom placed us in the chaos and
> darkness of the twentieth century as
>
> > poets and singers
> > engineers and schoolmasters
> > scholars and pastors
> > tailors and gardeners
> > builders and administrators
> > artists and lovers.
>
> Your Divine Providence called us into the company
> of your son Jesus. Therefore, we devote all our

energies to your Divine Majesty to bring order into our world, to make it fertile, and to bless it. We pledge you the hours of our lives and the use of our deaths through our Mother, the Lady Mary, and through our King and Good Brother, Jesus. Amen.

—Louis J. McCabe, SJ and Philip G. Steele, SJ

Litany of Contradictory Things

Wheat and weeds:
  let them grow together.

Arabs and Jews in Palestine:
  let them grow together.

Greeks and Turks of the Balkans:
  let them grow together.

Catholics and Protestants of Northern Ireland:
  let them grow together.

Pros and Contras of Central America:
  let them grow together.

Documented and undocumented aliens:
  let them grow together.

Immigrants and Native Americans:
  let them grow together.

Blacks and Whites of South Africa:
  let them grow together.

Sikhs and Hindus of India:
    let them grow together.

Revolutionaries and reactionaries:
    let them grow together.

Russians and Americans:
    let them grow together.

Religious leaders who lay and lighten burdens:
    Let them grow together.

Disciples prone to boasts and betrayals:
    let them grow together.

People of God who wound and heal:
    let them grow together.

Rich and poor, humble and haughty:
    let them grow together.

Those whose thinking is similar and contrary:
    let them grow together.

Those whose feelings are transparent or concealed:
    let them grow together.

Days of sparseness and days of plenty:
　　let them grow together.

Winter, spring, summer, fall:
　　let them grow together.

All the seasons of one's life:
　　let them grow together.

Joys and sorrow, laughter, tears:
　　let them grow together.

Strength and weakness:
　　let them grow together.

Doubt and faith:
　　let them grow together.

Denial and commitment:
　　let them grow together.

Preoccupation and freedom:
　　let them grow together.

Virtue and vice:
　　let them grow together.

Contemplation and action:
    let them grow together.

Giving and receiving:
    let them grow together.

The helpful and the helpless:
    let them grow together.

Wisdom of the East and West:
    let them grow together.

All contrarieties of the Lord:
    let them grow together.

—MICHAEL MOYNAHAN, SJ

Ignatian Litany of the Names of Jesus

The following litany is composed of various names St. Ignatius used for Jesus in his letters and other writings.

Jesus, Son of the Virgin, ... *Have mercy on us.*
Jesus, our Creator and Lord, . . .
Jesus, eternal Lord of all things, . . .
Jesus, who created and redeemed us, . . .
Jesus, who is to be our eternal judge, . . .
Jesus, divine majesty, . . .
Jesus, complete and perfect goodness, . . .
Jesus, infinite love, . . .
Jesus, our kindly Lord, . . .
Jesus, infinite wisdom, . . .
Jesus, author and source of every blessing, . . .
Jesus, the giver of every gift, . . .
Jesus, our perfect and eternal good, . . .
Jesus, our salvation, . . .
Jesus, our help and support, . . .
Jesus, our Mediator, . . .
Jesus, the power of God, . . .
Jesus, our supreme leader and Lord, . . .
Jesus, our food and companion in pilgrimage, . . .
Jesus, beautiful and lovable, . . .
Jesus, poor and humble, . . .

Jesus, made obedient for our sake, . . .

Jesus, plunged in sorrow, . . .

Jesus, overwhelmed by anguish and grief, . . .

Jesus, naked upon the cross, . . .

Jesus, who wished to be sold to redeem us, . . .

Jesus, who chose a painful death to give us eternal
life, . . .

Jesus, now in glory, . . .

Jesus, full of happiness and joy, . . .

Jesus, our consoler, . . .

Jesus, our peace, . . .

Jesus, our joy, . . .

Jesus, our hope, . . .

Jesus, our life, . . .

Jesus, our reward exceedingly great, . . .

Jesus, true life of the world, . . .

Jesus, our model and guide, . . .

Jesus, the head of your body the church, . . .

Jesus, the bridegroom of the church your
spouse, . . .

Jesus, your Father has placed us with you, . . .

Jesus, we have cast the anchor of our hope in
you, . . .

Jesus, move our hearts to follow you in complete
poverty, . . .

Jesus, help us conform to the will of the most Holy
    Trinity, . . .
Jesus, be the means of our union with the most
    Holy Trinity, . . .

Blessed be the name of Jesus, now and forever.
    Amen.

The Novena of Grace in Honor of St. Francis Xavier

St. Francis Xavier evangelized the Indies and Japan during ten years of extraordinary missionary activity beginning in 1542. A second St. Paul, he was canonized March 12, 1622, and named Patron of All Foreign Missions by Pope Pius X in 1904.

The Novena of Grace was prompted by the cure of Father Marcellus Mastrilli in 1634. At the point of death from a brain injury, he was cured instantaneously through the intercession of St. Francis Xavier, and afterward died a martyr in Japan.

The wonderful favors, both spiritual and temporal, which have been obtained through this novena have caused it to become known as the Novena of Grace. It is celebrated in many churches in all parts of the world from March 4 to March 12, the anniversary of the canonization of St. Francis Xavier. It may also be made at other times. This version of the novena is composed so that it can be used within the eucharistic liturgy at the times of the Prayer of the Faithful and the Thanksgiving after Communion.

Prayer of the Faithful

Celebrant: We have come together to worship the Lord our God and to honor the memory of his great-souled missionary St. Francis Xavier. Through his powerful intercession let us pray for ourselves, for the missionary efforts of the church, and for all the people of God.

Lector: For missions and missionaries throughout the world, that through the proclamation of the good news of salvation all may come to know the one true God and Jesus Christ whom God has sent. Let us pray to the Lord.

All: *Lord, hear our prayer.*

Lector: For the church, that renewed by the Holy Spirit, she may show forth to the world the mystery of the Lord and be an instrument of redemption for all. Let us pray to the Lord.

All: *Lord, hear our prayer.*

Lector: For Christian unity, that the Spirit of Christ, dwelling in all who believe, may bring us to that fullness of unity which Jesus desires—one Lord, one faith, one baptism. Let us pray to the Lord.

All: *Lord, hear our prayer.*

Lector: For the unrepentant, that moved by God's loving mercy revealed in Jesus, they may repent their sins and open their hearts to the divine life of grace. Let us pray to the Lord.

All: *Lord, hear our prayer.*

Lector: For ourselves, that we may be ever faithful to our baptismal commitment to Christ, and bring Christ's word and Christ's love to the world in which we live. Let us pray to the Lord.

All: *Lord, hear our prayer.*

Celebrant and People: Lord God, our Father, we honor the memory of the apostle of the Indies and Japan, St. Francis Xavier. The remembrance of the favors with which you blessed him during life and of his glory after death fills us with joy; and we unite with him in offering to you our sincere tribute of thanksgiving and of praise.

We ask you to grant us, through his powerful intercession, the inestimable blessing of living and dying in the state of grace. We also ask you to grant us the favors we seek in this novena.

(Pause to mention the spiritual or temporal favor you wish to receive.)

But if what we ask is not for the glory of God and the good of our souls, grant us, we pray, what is more conducive to both. We ask this through Christ our Lord. Amen.

Novena Prayer of Thanksgiving after Communion

Celebrant and People:
We give you thanks, O Lord,
for all your wondrous gifts.

We thank you for the gift of life:
you called us into being
that we might be your children
and live with you forever.

We thank you for our baptism:
you sealed us with the Holy Spirit,
gifted us with your own life,
grafted us into the mystical body of your divine
    Son.

We thank you for our vocation
to join with the risen Christ in working
to save and sanctify the world in which we live.

We thank you for this Eucharist:
you have fed us on the Bread of Life,
strengthened our faith,
renewed our hope,

deepened our love,
made us one with one another
in the Body of Christ, our Lord.

We give you thanks, O Lord,
for all your wondrous gifts. Amen.

This version of the Novena of Grace has been circulated by the Jesuit Seminary and Mission Bureau of the New Orleans Province.

My Mother

Holy Mary, my Queen, I recommend myself
to your blessed protection and special keeping,
and to the bosom of your mercy,
today and every day and at the hour of my death.
My soul and my body I recommend to you.
I entrust to you my hope and consolation,
my distress and my misery, my life and its
    termination.
Through your most holy intercession
and through your merits may all my actions
be directed according to your will and that of your
    Son.
Amen.

—St. Aloysius Gonzaga, SJ

Mary, My Advocate

Holy Mary, Virgin Mother of God,
I choose you this day
to be my queen, my patroness, and my advocate,
and I firmly resolve never to leave you,
and never to say or do anything against you,
nor ever permit others to do anything against your
    honor.
Receive me, then, I beg of you, for your servant
    forever.
Help me in my every action,
and abandon me not at the hour of my death. Amen.

—St. John Berchmans, SJ

For My Parents

O God, whom we obey in honoring our parents,
look down mercifully, I beseech you, on those
to whom in your providence I owe my being.
May they grow daily in faith, hope, and charity.
Implant deeply in their hearts the conviction
that as you are the beginning of all things
so to you must all return.
Condone their frailties,
pardon whatever excessive indulgence for me
they may have shown,
and impute not to them my waywardness,
my sloth, my weakness of will.
Grant them health and prosperity while life lasts,
pour upon them the abundance of your grace.
Defend and preserve them by your all-powerful hand.
May my Christian life,
in meeting their fondest expectations
and fulfilling their hopes,
be the consolation of their last years.
May they die the death of the just.
May they pass quickly to their heavenly home,
and may I join them there,
their dutiful child for all eternity. Amen.

—Daniel A. Lord, SJ

Prayer of an Aging Jesuit

Dearest Lord, teach me to grow gracefully.
Help me to see that my community does me no
  wrong
when gradually it takes from me my duties;
when it no longer seems to seek my views.

Rid me of my pride in all the "wisdom" I have
  learned.
Rid me of the illusion that I am indispensable.

Help me in this gradual detachment from earthly
  things
to grasp the meaning of your law of time.

Teach me, in this turnover of work and workers,
to discern a striking expression of life's constant
  renewal
under the impulse of your providence.

And please, Lord, let me still be useful,
contributing to the world my optimism,
adding my prayers to the joyful fervor and courage
of those who now take their turn at the helm.

Let my lifestyle now become one of humble and
    serene
contact with the world in change,
shedding no tears for the past;
making of my human sufferings
a gift of reparation to all my brothers.

Let my leaving the field of action be simple and
    natural—
like a glowing, cheerful sunset.

Lord, forgive me if only now in my tranquility
I begin to know how much you love me,
how much you've helped me.

And now, finally, may I have a clear, a deep
    understanding of the joyful destiny you have
    prepared for me, guiding my every step from the
    first day of my life.
Lord, teach me to grow old . . . just so.

*This prayer first appeared in the newsletter of the Venice-Milan
province in May 1973. It has since been translated and widely
reprinted.*

Prayer for the Grace to Age Well

When the signs of age begin to mark my body
(and still more when they touch my mind);
when the ill that is to diminish me or carry me off
strikes from without or is born within me;
when the painful moment comes
in which I suddenly awaken
to the fact that I am ill or growing old;
and above all at that last moment
when I feel I am losing hold of myself
and am absolutely passive within the hands
of the great unknown forces that have formed me;
in all those dark moments, O God,
grant that I may understand that it is you
(provided only my faith is strong enough)
who are painfully parting the fibres of my being
in order to penetrate to the very marrow
of my substance and bear me away within yourself.

—Pierre Teilhard de Chardin, SJ

A Prayer for Vocations

Father,
in the name of Jesus,
through the power of your Spirit,
inspire men and women
to labor for your kingdom.

We especially ask you
through the intercession
of Mary, our Mother,
St. Ignatius, and all the saints,
to help the Society of Jesus
continue its service of your church.

May your will be done. Amen.

Acknowledgments

Alba House for the prayers on pages 120, 136, 138, and 150. *Journeying with the Lord* by Carlo Maria Martini © 1987. Reprinted with permission.

The Crossroad Publishing Company for the prayers by Karl Rahner, *Prayers for a Lifetime*, edited by Albert Raffelt. Copyright © 1984 by The Crossroad Publishing Company. Also for the prayers by Carlo Martini on pages 133 and 146 from *Women in the Gospels* by Carlo M. Martini. English translation copyright © St. Paul Publications, England 1989. Reprinted by permission of The Crossroad Publishing Company.

Doubleday for the prayers on pages 25, 53, 104, 138, 146, 147, and 154 by Anthony de Mello, *Wellsprings: A Book of Spiritual Exercises*, © 1986, and for the prayer on page 27 by

Anthony de Mello, *Taking Flight: A Book of Story Meditations*, © 1988.

Gujarat Sahitya Prakash for the prayers on pages xx and 75 by Carlo Maria Martini, *Abraham Our Father in Faith*, © 1992; and for the prayer on page 164 by X. Diaz del Rio, *Ever to Love and to Serve: Prayer Services on Ignatian Themes*, Copyright © 1990. Reprinted with permission.

Harcourt Brace Jovanovich for the prayer by Pierre Teilhard de Chardin on page 144 from *The Heart of Matter*, translated by René Hague © 1979.

HarperCollins Publishers for prayers by Pierre Teilhard de Chardin on pages 37, 111, and 178 from *The Divine Milieu*, copyright © 1960 by Wm. Collins Sons & Co., London, and Harper & Brothers, New York; and for the prayer on page 134 from *Writings in Time of War* by Pierre Teilhard de Chardin, translated by René Hague © 1968.

The Institute of Jesuit Sources and the authors for the prayers on pages 3 and 7 by David L. Fleming, *The Spiritual Exercises: A Literal Translation and a Contemporary Reading*, © 1978; and for the prayers on pages 5, 14, 21, 34, 64, 82, 86, and 154 by Joseph Tetlow, *Choosing Christ in the World*, © 1989 Institute of Jesuit Sources, St. Louis, Missouri 63108. Reprinted with permission.

Landmark Enterprises and the author for the prayers on pages 43, 44, and 135 by William Breault, *A Voice over the Water: An Invitation to Pray*, © 1993 Landmark Enterprises, Rancho Cordova, California 96570. Reprinted with permission.

The prayers on pages 16, 30, and 57 by John A. Veltri, *Orientations Vol 1*, © 1993 Loyola House. Reprinted with permission of the author.

Loyola University Press for the prayer on page 85 by John Eagan, *A Traveler toward the Dawn*, edited by William O'Malley, © 1990. Reprinted with permission.

Oxford University Press for the poem on page 128 by Gerard Manley Hopkins, *The Poetical Works of Gerard Manley Hopkins*, edited by Norman H. MacKenzie © 1990 (1992) by permission of Oxford University Press on behalf of the Society of Jesus.

The Paulist Press for the prayers on pages 55, 76, 78, and 160 by Michael Moynahan, the prayer on page 28 by Leo Rock, and the prayer on page 94 by Stephen Privett from *Orphaned Wisdom: Meditations for Lent*, © 1990; and for the poem on page 47 by David J. Hassel, *Radical Prayer*, © 1983. Reprinted with permission.

The Macmillan Company for the poem on page 100 by Daniel Berrigan, *The World for Wedding Ring: Poems by Daniel Berrigan*, © 1962 Macmillan Company. Reprinted with permission of the author.

The Seabury Press for the prayers on pages 10, 11, 96, 112, and 143 by Daniel Berrigan, *Uncommon Prayer: A Book of Psalms,* © 1978. Reprinted with permission of the author.

The litany on pages 155–59 by Louis McCabe and Philip Steele is previously unpublished. It is published here with their permission, © 1993.

The prayer on page 152 by John J. Morris is reprinted with the author's permission.

Geoffrey Chapman Ltd. for the prayers on pages 71, 93, and 127 by St. Alphonsus Rodriguez, *St. Alphonsus Rodriguez: Autobiography,* translated by William Yeomans, SJ, © 1964.

Herder and Herder for the prayer on page 46 by Daniel A. Lord, *Letters to My Lord,* edited by Thomas Gavin, © 1969.

Burns & Oates for the prayer on page 116 by Jean-Pierre de Caussade, *Self-Abandonment to Divine Providence,* © 1959.

The prayer on page 149 by St. Ignatius of Loyola, *The Spiritual Legacy of Pedro Arrupe, SJ,* © 1985. New York Province of the Society of Jesus.

The prayers on pages 89 and 115 by Pedro Arrupe, *The Spiritual Legacy of Pedro Arrupe, SJ,* © 1985. New York Province of the Society of Jesus.

The prayer on page 147 by Pierre Teilhard de Chardin, *Let Me Explain*, texts selected and arranged by Jean-Piere Demoulin, translated by René Hague and others, © 1972, 1970. Reprinted with permission of Harper & Row.

The prayer on page 117 by Ignacio Martín-Baró, *Acción e ideología-psicología social desde Centroamerica* 2nd edition, © 1985. Reprinted with permission of UCA Editoras.

The prayer on page 88 by St. Ignatius of Loyola, *Letters of St. Ignatius of Loyola*, translated by William J Young, © 1959. Reprinted with permission of Loyola University Press.

The prayer on page 107 by Pierre Teilhard de Chardin, *Ad Majorem Dei Gloriam: A Collection of Prayers, Pictures and Poems for Friends of the Jesuits*, © 1979. Reprinted with permission of Oregon Province Jesuit Seminary and Mission Bureau.

The prayer on page 83 by St. Robert Southwell, *Place Me With Your Son*, © 1986. Reprinted with permission of Maryland Province.

Authors

Edmund Arrowsmith (1585–1628) labored as a priest for ten years in Lancashire, England, before he became a Jesuit. He later spent another five years ministering there before being arrested for being a priest. He wrote this offering of himself as he awaited execution on the scaffold.

Pedro Arrupe (1907–91) was the superior general of the Society of Jesus from 1965 to 1983.

John Berchmans (1599–1621) entered the Society of Jesus at the age of seventeen. During his brief life he quickly gained a reputation for being observant and faithful to his religious duties and his studies.

Daniel Berrigan has labored to raise consciousness about various moral issues through his writings and public demonstrations.

William Breault is a writer and artist who resides in California. He has published several books of prayerful reflections.

Edmund Campion (1540–81), known for his eloquent writing and poetry, exercised his priestly ministry in England for only thirteen months before being captured, tortured, and executed on a trumped-up charge of treason.

Peter Canisius (1521–97), who was sent by Ignatius to be a theological consultant at the Council of Trent, was appointed provincial superior of the Jesuits in Germany. Various catechisms of his enjoyed some two hundred printings during his lifetime and continued to be reprinted into the nineteenth century.

Peter Claver (1580–1654), who was encouraged by the advice of Alphonsus Rodriguez to volunteer to work in the Americas, spent the remainder of his life in Cartagena (in present-day Colombia) teaching and ministering to the African slaves, of whom he is said to have baptized over 300,000.

Jean-Pierre de Caussade (1675–1751) did spiritual direction, particularly through his writings, for the Visitation, Good Shepherd, and Poor Clare Nuns of Nancy and Albi in France.

John Eagan (1925–87) kept a journal while he taught at Marquette University High School, in which this intimate prayer was written.

Peter Faber (1506–46) was one of the original companions of St. Ignatius. Ignatius considered Faber most gifted in directing the Spiritual Exercises.

David L. Fleming is a former provincial superior of the Jesuits in the Missouri Province and the editor of *Review for Religious*, a bimonthly journal of spirituality.

John Futrell is an author and lecturer on Ignatian spirituality.

Aloysius Gonzaga (1568–91) came from a noble background to become a Jesuit. During his studies he begged alms for the plague-stricken and worked directly with the sick. He died after becoming infected with the disease.

David J. Hassel (1923–92) taught philosophy at Loyola University in Chicago. His books on prayer are appreciated by a wide audience.

Gerard Manley Hopkins (1844–89) spent part of his brief life teaching classics in Ireland, but he is best known for his intense poetry.

Claude La Colombière (1641–82) was the spiritual director of St. Margaret Mary Alacoque, whose visionary understanding of the love Jesus has for us was the foundation of the devotion to the Sacred Heart of Jesus.

Daniel A. Lord (1888–1955) was an indefatigable pamphlet-
eer who was also well known for his work with youth.

Ignacio Martín-Baró was one of the six Jesuits murdered along
with their cook and her daughter at the University of Central
America in San Salvador on the morning of November 16, 1989.
In their writings and teaching these Jesuits spoke out for justice
for the oppressed and voiceless of the world.

Cardinal Carlo Maria Martini is the archbishop of Milan. He
has been professor of Holy Scripture at the Biblical Institute
and rector of the Gregorian University in Rome.

Louis McCabe and **Philip Steele** have taught for many years
in Jesuit high schools. Both have also served as executive
assistants for the provincial. They prepared this litany for a
gathering of Missouri Province Jesuits. It can easily be
adapted for use in other places by simply changing the city
names and the specific jobs mentioned.

Jean-Pierre Médaille assisted a group of French women in
establishing the congregation of the Sisters of St. Joseph
in 1648. He based their rule, from which the two prayers in
this book are taken, on the Spiritual Exercises and the
Constitutions of the Society of Jesus.